OTHER WORKS BY ANTHONY CARINHAS

The Sorrow's Garden

The Vineyard Dregs

anthony CARINHAS

NEUROSIS

A Novel

autonomous publications

Life and death, energy and peace. If I stop today, it was still worth it. Even the terrible mistakes that I made and would unmake if I could. The pains that have burned and scarred my soul. It was worth it. For having been allowed to walk where I've walked—which was to hell on earth, heaven on earth, back again, into, under, far in-between, through it, in it, and above.

—Gia Carangi

Good times for a change
See the luck I've had
Can make a good man turn bad

So please please please
Let me, let me, let me
Let me get what I want this time

Haven't had a dream in a long time
See the life I've had
Can make a good man bad

So for once in my life
Let me get what I want
Lord knows it would be the first time

—The Smiths

For the Resistance

I

WHET

I am soul, mind, entity, and demon.
I'm unrivaled.
It's you reader that I tell a story of injustice.
Prove how I was tricked into thinking I was filth—and nothing more.
Do not abandon me on this journey to hell—for this is how it happened:

Saturday, April 19, 2008: 9.00 a.m.

I watched a towel spread bubbling foam across the window. The nametag read "Julie" and concern was creased on her forehead. I imagined what her troubles were as the American flag swayed in the distance.

Organic fair-trade coffee steamed between my hands as people walked behind her. *Julie* eventually came in with beads of sweat on her forehead, but that didn't stop her from asking, "Is there anything I can get you?"

It was strange that I knew her name even though I was just another face in the crowd.

"Not at the moment, thank you," I replied while stirring my coffee.

Her bright, hazel eyes burned from the distance. They revealed a damaged innocence capable of achieving her dreams, but couldn't due to the lack of advancement. The job may not have required much skill, but at least she was performing her duties for the sake of something better.

She began wiping tables in preparation for people who'd never worked slave-wage jobs before. They never appreciated the cleanliness, yet always expected it. If the girl wasn't wearing a smile like a machine, they were quick to write complaints.

I took the paper that headlined "Is the Economy in a recession?" The question had validity, but was anyone listening?

Halfway through the article, a hand pressed my shoulder.

"Is anyone sitting here?" asked the man with a scratchy voice.

I smiled and gestured toward the solitary chair.

"Please—I don't own the place."

He sat down and darted his eyes about the room. He wore a white beard with pale-blue eyes. His eyebrows were bushy with tiny eyes that could cut you with insult.

"It's ten in the morning and people are already giving me the eye of inconvenience."

The comment made me smile.

"It's never too early to ruin someone's morning. That should be expected these days."

He looked at the paper and placed a heavy finger at it. "Anything worth reading?"

I slid the paper toward him.

"Considering the president can't utter the word *recession*—the middle class withering—and unemployment skyrocketing. What's there to discuss?"

Three chairs down, a man leaned back and intensely glared at me. I presume my comment irritated him, but when the man I was conversing with turned to see what I was looking at, the stranger with black framed glasses and fresh shaven skin leaned forward. He pretended to read the paper, but it was obvious the man in his mid-forties continued listening.

Outside, a dog owner let her dog urinate in the flowerbed beside the café. She pretended not to notice as she scrolled through her phone because she presumably thought everyone was too busy to care. Her expensive jogging gear was most likely bought using her husband's paycheck since she was a stay-at-home wife.

"Would you look at that," I said.

"The nerve of some people."

He swept through several pages before his finger lifted with a type of tension that seemed consequential.

"My wife and grandkids weren't able to plan our usual vacation this year because the economy has been so stubborn. My family's never experienced that before," said the man.

A young couple walked in afloat with laughter.

"The decline will continue well into the New Year," I said.

"How unfortunate," said the man with a sigh. "But on a different note, sure is nice to have fifty-five degree weather in April."

"Winter comes later every year," as I sipped my French roast. "Did you order anything?"

"I had the barista make a fresh batch because she only had dark roast and I wanted a blond one."

Every coffee drinker enjoys fresh coffee, but asking for a fresh batch when the place was busy with one staff member was inconsiderate.

The barista with curly black hair approached the table and produced the man's cup.

"Is there anything *more* I can get you, sir?"

The derogatory sarcasm hung in her tone, but it was justified considering her pay wasn't enough to cater to such people on a daily basis.

He didn't look at her when he said, "No."

She shuffled away and apologized to the people in line. The café had become crowded, and it was interesting that the girl was the only person with a name in the nameless crowd.

"You must like your coffee black?" I asked.

He tapped the ceramic glass with the spoon and placed it on the napkin.

"If anyone's going to drink coffee—it must be black."

As he drank, he coarsely slurped the liquid. I looked about the room for prying eyes, but everyone pretended nothing was happening.

Deeply embarrassed, I pushed my chair in.

"It was nice meeting you."

He took his cup and replied, "You as well," and began slurping again.

Outside, a breeze rustled the trees as a group of laughing students walked by. It was ten in the morning and the day would fade just as it began.

On route to an upper-crust outdoors shopping center. There was no escaping the billboards that advertised sex-enhancement drugs, weight-loss pills, breast augmentations, artificial tanning, cellulite correction, and hair removal. The pictures littered the highway like a debilitating disease, yet the disease had become such a norm that the only way to cure it was to make more propaganda.

When I arrived, a group of girls no older than sixteen ran through the crowd yelling, "The new Juicy Couture is here," and vanished into the store. I looked around to see if anyone noticed the commotion, but indifference stained the crowd.

The premise of our story arrived when he appeared like a mirage from the crowd. His skin was like milk and his lips the color of blood. He moved with confidence and his body created an image too raw to describe. His eyes called with mysticism as he moved through the glass doors.

I couldn't decide whether to pursue the challenge, but the more his eyes burned in mind—the excitement called.

Inside the store, an army of sales men and women wore three-piece suits. The agony was unmistakable in their faces as they trolled the sales floor.

The marble floors reflected the flat screens advertising false vices. The twenty-foot ceiling

loomed like a cathedral above polished chrome
fixtures that shined with deceit.

"Would you care for a sample of our acai
fruit smoothie?" asked the sensual girl with a tray
of assorted cups.

I declined and continued my quest.

Jimmy Choos echoed through the
designer-scented air while texting occupied
the hands of overly tanned girls with poor skin
wearing Bottega Veneta sunglasses with clothing
that revealed tramp-stamp tattoos.

I sifted through tables and clothing racks
until I stumbled upon a Raf Simons shirt for the
evening. I moved toward the dressing rooms when
a young girl with straight black hair and thick eye
makeup approached me. She smelled sweet, as
her heels suited her seductive demeanor. She was
lucky enough to not be a part of the two million
people who'd lost their jobs since January.

She took the shirt and placed it on a silver
rack inside the room.

"I'll be back in five minutes to see how
things are going!"

Hip-hop music filled the rooms as I undressed. The lyrics foreshadowed that the end times were upon us.

The mirror embodied a blue light as I undressed. It turned my green eyes teal as I removed the shirt from the hanger. It flattered my arms and stomach since I spent considerable time at the gym. Weightlifting was a hobby of mine since high school, but now that I was older, the lifestyle kept my skin and physique youthful.

Satisfied with the shirt, I opened the door and the ambitious girl quickly asked, "How did everything work out?"

"I think I'll take it."

"Are we ready to check out then?"

"Not at the moment. But when I am. I'll let you know."

My thoughts were elsewhere when I turned the corner and crashed into the fellow I was looking for.

I imagined his bare flesh upon me, but I cleared my thoughts.

"Sorry for that. Guess I need to pay more attention."

"Do you do that often?" he said loudly.

"On occasion."

His seductive eyes roared with delight.

"You're quite good at it. Now I see why you did it."

"I wouldn't go that far," I said jokingly. "I'm here on a mission."

It felt as if my apprehension were transparent.

"So that means you're here to scope out the competition to develop a complex?"

A group of guys whose legs and arms were decorated with tattoos talked about their weekend of promiscuity and drug use as they passed by.

"I'm afraid a complex is the least of my concerns," he said.

We passed a row of girls receiving complimentary makeovers when a voice cried from the crowd, "Do me like Lana Turner!"

In the interim, I noticed that I was taller than him, but I liked that. One could also see he spent a substantial amount of time in the sun because he was more bronze than me.

"By the way, my name is Christian," I said politely.

He held out his hand.

"Nice to meet you. I'm Gregory."

"Are you here with anyone?"

"Just my parents and visiting brother."

"That's nice. Where's he visiting from?"

"The University of Toronto."

"Really? That's quite an accomplishment."

"I know."

"I remember when me and a close friend went abroad for school. We did a year at the University in Zürich."

"Wow. I hope you went to the museums."

"I did. I even got to see Warhol's Campbell's Soup Can."

Gregory smirked to the idea swimming in this head.

"My family's taken us to Europe twice, but we never went to Switzerland. Every time we go I never want to come back," said Gregory.

"Their way of life is different. More introspective."

"Yes. I thought the same thing. If I could live there now, I would."

"You should spend a semester abroad then," I said.

"I wouldn't be able to."

"How come?"

"I still have two years till college."

Bewilderment consumed me.

"Oh."

After my reaction, he replied, "So I'm a junior. Get over it."

"Yes. But—"

"But what? We're talking now, aren't we?"

The knot in my throat felt ever so present as I looked around.

"I think—"

"That you should stop being paranoid."

"That isn't as easy as it sounds."

"So you want me to leave then?"

"Well, not this instant."

"See. I knew you wouldn't think anything of it."

His nonchalant attitude calmed me when he smiled.

"I'm sorry for that. But what were we talking about?" I asked.

"Traveling—silly."

"Of course. And where was it you wanted to go?"

"Germany."

"Why there?" I said.

"After reading *The Magic Mountain* and *Steppenwolf.* It sort of gave me ideas."

He rolled his eyes when his phone began ringing.

After the conversation, he placed the phone in his pocket.

"My brother wants to meet at the Apple store," replied Gregory.

"Buying an iPhone, I presume?"

"Yeah. He's taking advantage of the situation and my parents always take the bait."

"I'm sure it's nothing like that," I said.

"That may be. But I'm tired of shopping and want lunch."

"I feel famished myself," taking a peek at my watch. "I think I've kept you long enough. Your brother's probably wondering where you are."

"He can wait," as Gregory pulled the phone from his pocket. "What's your number by the way?"

"Why would you want that?"

"If you're seeing someone. I understand."

"Ha. If anything, that would be you," I said.

"So what's the number, Christian?"

Floored by the proposal, his playful nature provoked me like a thorn. I understood the boundaries I would cross as I debated my thoughts. It was a proposal I'd never encountered before, but it seemed harmless. So after we moved to the registers to purchase our items, we went outside.

"Well, it was nice meeting you," said Gregory as he put on his sunglasses.

"Same here."

"Maybe we can do something soon."

"I would like that," I said.

He smiled as a gust of wind rustled through the trees. But before I could blink, he disappeared into the throng around us.

II

LIGHTS

Saturday, April 19, 2008: 8.00 p.m.

Evening washed the sky as I drove through the tranquil darkness. My friend John had much to discuss over dinner. His weekend visit from Cambridge produced a memorable evening. His dark brown hair was neatly combed and his blue collared shirt matched his tan loafers. He still moved with a polished stride as his white pants defined his legs. He was only thirty and he still looked youthful.

Several hours passed and soon the conversation took a different tone.

"When Mathieu was diagnosed with pancreatic cancer, the premiums doubled. We couldn't afford the treatments or medications anymore. You can imagine what came next," he said somberly.

Grief clenched me.

"You should've called for help," I said.

"It's how he wanted things."

"I know. But if there was anything I could've done."

"It just got really tough at the end. But somehow I managed."

"What did you do to keep yourself from going crazy?"

His green eyes moved as if seeking escape.

"I went back to get my doctorate in English."

"How's that coming along?"

"I only have two more classes."

"I take it you know what you're going to do afterwards."

"Not entirely. But academic administration sounds intriguing."

"I'm sure Mathieu would've liked that."

"He would've because he knew how much I missed academia after I left that teaching post with Harvard."

"How long did you do that?"

"Two years while I was in grad school."

"I see," bringing the glass to my lips. "Wasn't that where you met?"

"Yeah. He was working on publishing an article in biomedical engineering when we met in the library." He paused but refrained from receding too far in his thoughts. "So much promise—and to have everything taken from you at thirty-two is devastating."

"I agree. At least you got married before things got bad."

"It was the last major event he got to enjoy."

"I hope you didn't mean that cynically."

"No. If anything—at least I'm getting a second chance."

After dinner, I accompanied John to his car.

I reached for his shoulder and said, "I'm glad you called. We should do this more often."

The embrace filled our eyes with tears.

"And that's what makes this so hard. I didn't want to do this alone."

"I know. But you loved one another. You honored his requests as much as possible. So now you can breathe."

"Now that I have so much time on hand. It feels strange."

"Like I said, you're welcome anytime."

"Will do. Good-bye, Christian."

Driving home, my mind sank into a realm of gloom. Death wasn't an easy subject to discuss. Mathieu was special and his demeanor was always refined. Even though he came from a wealthy family with a lineage from Harvard. He was modest and never complained about anything.

Reality receded from my thoughts when the phone rang. My heart stopped when I saw that it was Gregory.

"Hello?"

"Are you busy," he asked.

"No. I just got done with dinner. You?"

"What would you say if I wanted to see you tonight?"

The bottle of wine Mathieu and I consumed made Gregory's voice angelic. "Wouldn't you rather be with your friends?" "They're old news." "I'll take that as a compliment," I said with a laugh. "You want to head over when I get home?" "Can you get me if I text you the address?" "What about your parents?" "Don't worry. Everyone's in their rooms already." "I need to stop at my place first. Give me twenty minutes." "All right. Call when you're in the neighborhood." When I arrived at my building, traces of Chanel No. 8 lingered in the corridor. The weekend night life was always vibrant in the building. The perfume recalled the times I used to be out until sunrise a few years ago. How I'd sleep the entire day just to do it again the following night. It made sense why people worked for the weekend because there was no better bond than conversing with strangers.

A voice lurked from around the corner and stared at me.

"Good evening, Mr. Wall. Having a pleasant evening?" asked the voice.

The women had retired from walking the dog in the courtyard.

"Good evening, Mrs. Campbell. You look dashing tonight. How are you?"

"Bert and I had the most exquisite dinner at the Hyatt Hill Country Resort just now."

"Haven't seen him lately. How is he?"

"Good. The Board has been busy lately."

"What is Tesoro digging around for now?"

"They're in the process of acquiring three hundred existing wholesale supply contracts with Shell."

World domination had no interest to me, so I blew smoke up her ass to watch her gloat.

"Impressive."

"Tonight was our first night out in weeks."

Her magenta jacket with large black buttons squeezed her tiny waist. Her thin blonde hair was wavy from morning curlers, but it only emphasized her thin eyebrows, nose, and lips.

"I'm sure you'll have more in the future," I said.

A demonic grin consumed her face.

"Are you ready for the Pennsylvania primary?" she asked.

"I am."

"I'm sure she'll win."

"Anything is possible right now."

"I hope you're not defending Obama."

"His campaign raised more than forty million last month. That's quite a following."

"I don't see why. He's associated with people who were involved in the Weather Underground."

"The delegate race is really close right now. She's already lost most of super delegates, but we'll have a definitive answer by next month."

"Well, at least she doesn't have to go around begging for Jewish votes," she said nasally.

"People are entitled to their vote, Mrs. Campbell."

The dog started barking as she snapped to shush it.

"Funny how Obama claims to be a working-class man. Yet he can't get the working-class vote."

"If it's any consolation. He hasn't won a top ten state since February 5th."

"It needs to stay that way. But the media also needs to quit saying, 'What's in it for Hilary?' When I say, 'What's in it for Barack!'"

I took the bait and continued to see what else she would say.

"The media's always been biased," I said.

"His delusional campaign of *Change* leaves me sick. Propaganda at its best! I mean, the man can't even speak without a teleprompter. Is ineptitude that rampant at Harvard?"

"Mrs. Campbell. I would love to chat, but I have business to attend to."

She stomped her black patent leather shoe on the foot and her dachshund began to bark again.

"How could anyone vote for a candidate who doesn't wear an American flag lapel pin— especially after 9/11?"

The air grew sour.

"That could be brought into question. But he thinks patriotism is greater than displaying a symbol."

"What are his motives, Mr. Wall? Why would an unpatriotic person run for president? You out of all people should be the one defending the sovereignty of civil rights?"

"I agree. But right now that's not on people's minds."

"Well it needs to. If no one's going to preserve that—who will?"

Her animosity became claustrophobic.

I opened the door and hastily said, "Good night, Mrs. Campbell."

I watched through the peephole as she stared at the door. Her oval black eyeglasses bulged through the lens. Her magenta lips moved as she filled the hall with hot air.

"Our country is on the brink of collapse. That takes responsibility. You think a novice can do that, Mr. Wall? Someone who wasn't even born in the United States!"

She hysterically laughed as she moved down the hall. It was strange how being in your mid-forties could fill you with so much piss and vinegar.

I checked the phone to see where Gregory lived. The spontaneous event provoked me to assemble a plate of cheese in case we got hungry.

I switched off the light and locked the door.

The elevator parted and the night felt mysterious. I wasn't sure why my stomach felt knotted as I drove along the ten-mile journey.

I pulled into the neighborhood and called Gregory.

"Wait two houses down. I'll be out in a bit."

The street was wide and the houses were grand with dreamy landscapes that revealed their affluence. It was comforting to know he wouldn't be asking for money, but then again, that was to be determined since these were the type of kids who did the most drugs.

His shadow moved across the rearview mirror and his smile appeared at the door.

He moved onto the leather seat.

"Sorry. Thought my brother got up."

"If you can't come. There's no pressure."

"It's all right. I'm ready when you are."

I pulled the top down so the overhead lights could stream over us as we scurried down the highway. The white convertible Porsche moved like ecstasy on wheels.

"How was the rest of your day?" I asked.

"We didn't leave for another two hours after you left. But lunch was good." He grabbed his bag embellished with sown-on patches. "You mind if I put on some music?"

"Sure."

He linked his phone and soon screeching guitars blared toward the sky.

"Who is this?"

His magnetic eyes electrified the atmosphere. "This is my favorite song. 'Exercise One' by Joy Division."

Vibration rattled us as the wind tousled our hair. The song sent chills like a black widow crawling over my skin. It was unlike anything I'd heard—but it somehow settled my nerves.

When we arrived, the elevator parted and the corridor with red carpet, orange walls, and blue velvet chairs sat in stillness.

Loft 2679 opened to a red lamp perched on the piano. The north and east side of the living room had floor-to-ceiling windows that overlooked the city.

"Some view," Gregory said.

"Feel free to look around. I'll be back in a moment."

When I came back, Gregory was holding a silver frame.

"Is that your family?"

"Yeah. Turns out that friend I went to Zürich with is my ex-wife."

"Who old is your son?"

"Timothy is two."

"Do they live with you?"

"They visit from time to time, but Miranda and I decided it was best they stayed elsewhere."

"Sorry to hear that."

"It gave her the chance to remarry."

"Where did you meet her?"

"We were in the same history class at Columbia."

Gregory looked at the picture as if it were a thousand miles away as the clock ticked in the background.

"Does that mean you're happy now?"

I didn't find the questions offensive because I wasn't afraid of the truth.

"I couldn't hide from myself anymore. So in that respect, I am."

"Funny how love vanishes as quickly as it appears."

"You can't let that make you cynical. Always carry the benefit of doubt."

He turned toward the glimmering lights and said, "May I step on the terrace?"

"Make yourself at home. Would you like a glass of water?"

"Do you know how to make a black velvet?"

"I do."

"We should have one then."

I retreated from the kitchen and handed him a frothy mixture that swirled like a witch's broth. He leaned against the railing as sounds from below climbed the glass pillar. The collage of lights illuminated the distance.

"I like how you didn't let the truth scare
you," said Gregory.

"Sometimes you have to do what's right."

"My family cares for my brother and me
deeply. But over the years, I've begun to question
that."

"How so?"

"I feel as if they found out about me, they
would feel differently about me."

"If you told them the truth, and they turn
away. You've done nothing wrong."

Gregory's eyes touched from the distance.

"Maybe I should be honest like you were.
Just to see what happens."

"That's up to you. But I wanted everyone
to be free. Miranda was very accepting of the
circumstances."

"You got lucky she wasn't ignorant."

"People choose that label because it gives
them the excuse to be malicious."

"Such a waste of energy."

I looked at his glass.

"Would you care for another?"

"Yes."

I brought the carafe outside and filled our glasses. Gregory savored the taste and continued, "Do you remember how life was when you were a kid?"

"That's a peculiar question," I said.

"I know. But I'm trying to get at something."

"In what respect?"

"How you perceived life until betrayal changed you."

"Has someone done that to you recently?"

His face became slightly ridged. "My parents' *prescribed* love comes to mind."

"I see."

"I shouldn't feel trapped, but they make me feel that way."

"Are you certain they won't accept you?"

"My parents donate to the Koch Brothers."

I found the association discouraging because they're an extreme right-wing group that believes Social Security, Medicare, Medicaid, and public education in America should be eliminated. It made me realize he had reason to feel threatened.

"Now I see why you're hesitant," I said.

"We'll just see how things play out. But what about you? What was growing up like for you?"

"My parents died when I was nine. So my grandparents raised me."

"I'm sorry about that."

"It was such a long time ago. But being my grandparents weren't so progressive. They had high expectations about everything. Education was their biggest priority."

"Did they know about you?"

"Not until after the divorce."

"But didn't that take some of the pressure off your shoulders?"

"Not entirely," I said with a laugh. "How they found out wasn't the most orthodox way to deliver that sort of thing."

"I don't know. All this secrecy makes me want to run away sometimes."

"But where would you go?"

"San Francisco or New York."

"To do what?"

"I don't know. Anything, I guess."

"I wouldn't advise that."

"Why not?"

I chuckled and swigged at my drink.

"Because it's okay to be proud of your convictions. They'll reward you for your loyalty."

Gregory walked forward and pressed his lips against mine.

He opened his eyes and said, "It's five-thirty in the morning."

"Is it time to leave already?"

"My parents won't be up for another two hours."

The air hummed as his eyes sparkled against the night. It was odd how he hadn't asked what I did for a living. The interest to know who I was more than where I worked was peculiar. Most people pinned you on that before knowing your name. It made the circumstances all the more thrilling.

"We can leave whenever you like," I said.

"Another hour wouldn't hurt."

My pulse left me warm.

"Would you like something to eat?"

The question was disregarded.

"Where's your room?" he asked.

"Why?"

"You'll see."

We moved through the living room to the bedroom.

He pushed me on the bed and ran his tongue along my neck. The warmth was intense as his heart beat against me. His skin smelt like almond as I licked his stomach. I removed his clothing to find a well-defined body.

I wanted to pull back, but he somehow lured me to fulfill his desires.

I lifted him against the wall as his legs wrapped around me. The cries of ecstasy intensified the quicker I thrusted. It was priceless to watch him quiver because the thrill was genuine.

When the deed concluded. He looked at the clock with sweat glistening at his chest.

"We should get going," he said.

"Sure thing."

We got dressed and drove just as dawn broke the night.

III

SILVER

Friday, May 9, 2008: 7.00 a.m.

The Collinses' home had a white picket fence. A lawn of the greenest hue with enormous oak trees above the house and street. The shutters were yellow, and the paneling on the second floor was orange-red. The ivy along the base of the house covered the gray limestone.

Myrtle's hair was in a French twist as she read *The Reprieve*, by John Paul-Sarte. Sunlight passed through the floor-to-ceiling windows and transformed her white clothes into a glowing object.

She set the book aside when the front door opened.

Gregory and Nathan retired on the red leather sofa with eagerness.

Gregory leaned back and placed his arms beneath his head. "Where's Dad?"

"He's dropping clients off at the airport," replied Myrtle.

The trees rustled outside.

"Oh," said Gregory.

The house cat jumped on Nathan's lap. He ran his fingers through the fur as the purring massaged his hand.

"Any plans for the weekend?" asked Nathan.

"Your father would like to spend the weekend in Fredericksburg. But we won't know until you guys are on the road."

"That sounds like a grand idea."

"I thought so. We haven't gone out in a while because we've been so busy."

"There's no excuse for Dad not to take you out, though."

"Well, when you have your own business. You'll see how easy time slips away."

Sunlight rested on Gregory's legs as it glistened on his moisturized skin.

"If you go. Bring back some pear pie," added Nathan.

"Speaking of pies. I made some for your trip."

Their checks burned because it was their favorite.

"I was wondering why you were buzzing around in the kitchen so early." said Gregory.

"When you told me there wouldn't be school today. I decided to stay home and take advantage of the day," said Myrtle.

The front door opened and Josh stepped into the den.

He patted Gregory's head before sitting next to Myrtle.

"Are you guys packed?" he asked.

"We did that last night," said Gregory.

He looked at his boys with pride.

"Sounds good."

"What time did I say to be back on Sunday?" asked Myrtle.

"Not past midnight," replied Nathan.

"Be sure to call so we know when to expect you," added Josh.

Nathan knew they were putting the majority of responsibility on him since he was the eldest.

He smiled and pushed the cat from his lap.

"Sure thing," said Nathan.

Gregory stood up and said, "I'm going to get the cooler—"

"Leave it in the car. We'll stop at Whole Foods before the lake."

"All right."

Josh then reached into his coat and took out a lucky rabbit's foot.

"Here are the keys to the boat," his eyes burning as he stared at Nathan. "Under no circumstances shall you or Gregory drink! Am I being clear, young man?"

He swallowed the lump in his throat.

"Yes, sir."

"No speeding either," Myrtle replied with density.

"I know."

"Remember what I said," lifting an eyebrow.

"I won't pay for a second ticket," said Myrtle.

Nathan bent down and kissed his mother's forehead.

"Don't worry. I'll have everything under control."

Gregory moved to the doorway and put on his sandals.

"Thanks for renting the cabin, Dad."

They opened the door just as the clock chimed eight times.

♌

The lake glittered against the blazing sun.

The cries of laughing children echoed under the blue sky as families picnicked under the tress.

Pointing to the boat, Nathan narrowed his eyes and looked at Gregory.

"Did you put the sunscreen in the bag? Once we're gone—I'm not coming back for it."

Gregory closed the trunk with his forearm and squinted.

"I already double checked."

Gregory moved with a fishing hat, sunglasses, and ice chest in hand. The day was warm, but the lake prevented the heat from being overwhelming.

They moved along the deck as the ice rustled in the chest.

"Did you lock the cabin?" asked Nathan.

"Yes."

Gregory sat on the boat's edge and dipped his toe in the water. A plane passed overhead and its shadow fluttered on the ground as the children tried shooting it down with imaginary guns.

Nathan untied the rope and rubbed his hands with anticipation.

"All right, let's get this baby going."

The boat retreated from the dock and soon the hills were moving between them. Nathan closed his eyes and listened to the water ripple behind them.

They found a good place to idle so they could get their gear in order. It wasn't long until a boat approached with a young couple.

"You guys catch anything?" asked Nathan.

"We managed two one-pound catfishes," said the man with blond hair. His arms were tight with a firm stomach as the sunscreen made his body shiny.

"You all keep it or toss it back?" asked Gregory.

"We play for keeps. These guys will definitely be grilled tonight," said the woman with light brown hair in a two-piece bathing suit. Her breasts were large and her skin was bronze and toned.

The couple slowly put on the gas.

"Enjoy the rest of your day," they said.

"We will," replied Nathan.

Gregory reached into the chest and opened a bottle of Trilogy Kombucha. The hissing popped the cap as foam ran down his hand. Nathan sat up and reached into the ice chest.

"That sounds good," as he too licked the fizz with his tongue.

Nathan later removed his shirt and began to rub sunscreen over his body. Once his arms and shoulders were finished, he turned to his brother and said, "Will you get my back?"

The boat swayed from side the side as he moved his hands in circular motions. Once the substance was absorbed, he set the bottle down.

"There you are."

"Thanks. Let me know when you're ready."

Gregory opened the chest and removed a bag of bait before removing his shirt.

The cool lotion felt thick on his back as Nathan's hands felt therapeutic. The smell of the water and sunblock reminded him of when the four of them spent a week along Lake Travis during the summers. This was the first time they came alone because they wanted to spend the weekend together. Every time they came, their mother baked a pear pie, so it meant a lot to them that she remembered to do that.

"You're all set," said Nathan.

"Thanks."

They both took their fishing poles and loaded them with bait.

Gregory's forehead wrinkled as his upper lip curled and cast the hook forward.

Nathan turned and saw his reflection in Gregory's sunglasses.

"So is there anyone you're dating?" asked Nathan.

"Not really. I'm pretty focused on school right now."

"I thought you were sort of seeing Jeanie."

"What! No way. We've been friends since seventh grade. That would be weird."

"So that explains the closeness. I was just asking since you knew I still had time for girls when I was your age."

"I know. It was funny knowing those two girls were competing over you that year."

"I won four medals on the varsity track team that year. Of course that's going to draw attention."

"Are you still talking with that one you settled down with senior year?"

"Yeah. She's at UCLA studying journalism."

"Awesome."

"Yeah. She's already come out to visit during spring break."

"You never told me that."

"Since I live on campus downtown. We went to the CN Tower, art galleries, West Queen West neighborhoods, and went cycling around the Blue Flag beaches."

"Nice."

"I was supposed to spend the summer with Ruby at UCLA this summer. But Dad wouldn't let me. He said I needed to spend time with the family since you're going to be a senior next year."

"I guess they're feeling old."

"I thought the same thing. So I asked Dad if he was feeling that way. But he said once you leave for college, he's going to taking on more cases. You know how he gets the more free time he has."

"I know. Makes me wonder if we're going to be like that."

"That wouldn't be so bad."

"Does that mean you're going to law school?"

"No. I decided to do business. Seems more practical for me. Law seems stuffy, and I don't like that."

"Makes sense."

"So, are you going to stay on the swim team next year?" asked Nathan.

"Yeah. It really keeps me focused."

"What were the three golds you won at the state finals this year?"

"One for the 100-yard butterfly, 500-yard freestyle, and 100-yard backstroke."

"Nice. And none of the girls on the team are interested?"

Gregory began to feel awkward as it was only natural for brothers to talk about girls. As much as he wanted to tell Nathan about his homosexuality, he wasn't ready to be on the defense. He had just met Christian, so he was willing to see where things went before sharing his personal life.

"Not really. I've talked with a few of them, but no one's caught my attention," said Gregory.

"All right. I'm just trying to look after you."

"I know. I'm just ready for something different I guess."

"Why did you say that so passively? I still remember the summer before junior year thinking time was eternal and that nothing could stop me.

But sure enough when senior year rolls around, time accelerates with or without you."

"I'm sick of dealing with fickle acquaintances already. I want substance. And I feel college will do that for me," added Gregory.

"I know you're ready to meet new people, but be patient. You're going to look back and miss the simple life once college starts because everything gets complicated after that. Just know Mom and Dad gave us something even the most prestigious colleges can't teach, and that's understanding the value of responsibility."

"And that's what I want because every time you come home, life changes you somehow. It's noticeable how you've grown younger at heart but older in spirit." said Gregory.

"You'll experience that soon enough. Trust me," replied Nathan as he looked at his watch. "You ready to head back?"

"Sure."

When they arrived to the cabin. They took the pie from the fridge and topped it with vanilla ice cream. The sat on the porch and savored the dessert as they watched the sunset melt onto the landscape. The sky seemed to catch fire as the clouds drifted overhead.

Still hungry from the day, they washed up and decided to grab burgers by the food trailers down the road.

IV

CAPPUCCINO

Sunday, May 18, 2008: 7.00 a.m.

The alarm clock buzzed and Myrtle silenced it. She stared at the ceiling fan and inhaled deeply. Her husband slept beneath the pillow, and this always brought a smile to her drowsy but happy mornings.

She climbed out of bed to expose a nakedness that was firm and sensual. She heard from men in the past that her breasts were quite the pair. She stood at the mirror as she rubbed them because she agreed that she was an advertisement for perfection.

She entered the bathroom and ran the water until it was engulfed with steam. She washed her hair and body with essential oils. A process that exhilarated her because beauty was a priority.

Afterwards, she moved to the kitchen in a robe to prepare breakfast. Organic coffee beans were ground while the house cat rubbed her legs. She reached into the cupboard and poured organic grain-free pellets into its bowl.

She went upstairs and stood at the doorway as she watched her husband sleep. The carpet was soft as she moved toward the red drapes to draw them. The fog was still thick as it lingered over the grass.

She sat next to him and tenderly touched his cool back. "Josh. Josh, honey, it's time to wake up."

He moaned and stretched before opening his eyes. His eyes were a deep topaz and his beauty was truly unique.

"Is it time already? It seems like I just fell asleep."

Her fingers ran through his hair.

"It's eight-thirty," she said as she stood up. "The paper and coffee are ready downstairs."

Josh walked to the middle of the room and stretched. He looked at his naked reflection and admired the proportion of his chest, legs, and penis. His palm moved over his stomach as he turned sideways to see the contrast of his butt to his lower abdomen. He moved to the shower and lathered his body with a shea butter scrub. He then masturbated into his palm and ate his semen to invigorate himself.

He entered the kitchen in a gray robe and took a cinnamon raisin bagel. He spread organic cream cheese across it, then poured his coffee.

Myrtle's straight black hair made her jade eyes sparkle against fleshy red lips. Her flawless and supple skin radiated with youth—making it hard for anyone to guess her age.

Josh sat at the table and opened the paper.

"Anything interesting?" he asked.

"This Proposition 8 title is really gaining steam in California."

"Really? How so?"

"Its supporters want the state's Supreme Court to certify it so it can be on the November 4th ballot," replied Myrtle.

"That's great. Proposition 22 never should've been found unconstitutional."

"Well, if Prop. 8 passes. The provision will be cemented into the state's Constitution stating only a man and a woman can marry."

"Good. Massachusetts already grants these perverts a marriage license. So now California thinks they can do the same," said Josh dryly.

"I don't see why," replied Myrtle as she sipped her coffee. "They need to understand this has nothing to do with equality, but respecting a sacred tradition."

Josh lowered the paper and looked at Myrtle haughtily.

"People can protest all they want. But U.S. Supreme Court will never legalize it," said Josh.

"I hope not. I'm just thankful we don't have to worry about that sort of thing."

"No kidding. Our boys know better than to get involved with that type of junk."

She folded the paper and finished her coffee.

"Honey, I'll be upstairs getting ready," she said.

"I'll be up in a minute."

♌

For the past five years, Myrtle and Josh indulged at the Woodhouse Day Spa on Sundays. Its ambiance allowed its guests to feel like royalty so that thousands of dollars could be spent in hopes to escape the world.

A woman with long, thick golden hair no older than twenty-one greeted them.

"Good morning. Good to see you again," said the girl.

"Thank you, Gaby. How was your week?"

"It was wonderful. My fiancé and I found our dream home two weeks ago. The bank approved our loan on Friday."

"Congratulations. We hope the future will be bright for you both," replied Josh.

The attendant led them to a large stainless steel door and opened it. The couple kissed before departing to the changing area.

Once Josh was changed, he walked down the pink corridor to room Z. Three soy-free candles burned with cotton wicks at the counter. The lavender tamed his spirit as he removed the robe and lied on the massage table. He listened to the rainforest sounds that channeled through the speakers.

The masseur quietly came in and washed his hands at the sink. Mark was in his mid-twenties, stocky, and tanned. His hazel eyes complemented his manicured nails and lemon-cedar scented beard. He always admired Josh's body and couldn't wait to touch it. If Josh knew how Mark enjoyed the scent of his skin and hair before it was dressed with oil, he would've never let him touch him.

"Good morning, Josh. How is everything?"

"Well as always. And yourself?"

Eucalyptus, rosemary, avocado, and witch hazel oils were pulled from the cupboard. He mixed them and distributed them along his back while Josh watched the shadows on the wall.

"I'm well, considering some of the stories I've heard these past days," he said.

"Like."

Mark started with his lower back.

"When Eliot came in the other day for a deep Swiss. His mind wasn't in the best of places."

"He and I went to high school together. We don't talk much these days, but when we do, we catch up. What did he have to say?"

Gossip was the highlight of Mark's day because he enjoyed talking about things that weren't happening to him.

"Do you really want to know?"

"Yes."

"Eliot and Emily have been having marital problems and they agreed to see a psychotherapist. The therapist ruled Emily as having the heaviest burden, so he put her on Prozac and him on Viagra."

"I knew they were having problems, but going to a therapist is taking it to the next level," said Josh.

"I agree."

"What else did he say?"

"As the months lapped, they regularly attended their sessions and everything seemed fine until they had a really bad argument. Eliot swallowed a few Valiums, but it didn't help when he woke up to find the bed vacant. He wasn't sure why she was up at four in the morning, so he searched the house—but it was empty. When he checked the garage, the car was on when he found her unconscious with her wrists slashed."

"What an awful thing for Eliot to see. He's one of the most sensitive people I know."

"Eliot never shied away from speaking his mind, and he was always a pleasure to be around."

"That sounds accurate."

"Would you like to hear the rest of the story?"

"Sure," said Josh.

"Their psychotherapist came to the hospital that night to detain her in the psych ward for further monitoring. Eliot blamed himself because the kids blamed him for the incident. A few days later a letter was addressed to the children. Perplexed by it, Eliot called the doctor asking why the letter wasn't screened."

"That's odd. I can't image her saying something horrible."

"Well, apparently it said she was never going to see the children again when her release date was scheduled in a few days. Later that day, the family received word that she committed suicide by logging a plastic knife in her throat."

Josh didn't like to think he was superior over others, but he felt he always had a better head on his shoulders. He didn't understand how a marriage could fail because everything in life required work.

"The poor man. I had no idea he was having so such trouble. I just saw him a month ago and everything seemed okay. He's always been a good man who loved his family more than anything. How unfortunate," said Josh.

Forty-five minutes had passed and Mark put heated rocks on Josh's back for the remaining fifteen minutes.

"I'll be back to wake you."

Meanwhile, Myrtle moved from the massage session to the nail salon.

She was greeted by Melissa, who was twenty-nine but looked no older than twenty.

She had red lipstick, brown hair, black nails, and hazel eyes.

"Myrtle, if it isn't you. I've been expecting you."

Myrtle tossed her hair aside with a smile.

"Ever since I started getting these massages. I don't know how I survived all these years without them."

Melissa took her foot and washed it with a towel.

"That's what everybody says."

"Do you get them often?" asked Myrtle.

"Are you kidding? Everyone here uses their discount."

"If I recall, you've been here two years?"

"Yes."

"You must enjoy this, then."

"It's a good stepping stone. But clients have intriguing stories."

"You must find me boring then since I never have anything substantial to talk about" said Myrtle with a snort.

"Oh no. I wouldn't say that. We talk about all sorts of things."

"Is there something you would like to share?"

"Do you recall that woman who used to hurry in after you?"

"Yes. What a strange person she was. I haven't seen her for a while. Did she stop coming?"

"Yes."

"How come?"

"Her name was Stacy and she suddenly took her daughter, Amy, out of school."

"Oh. I imagine something must've happened for that to have happened," said Myrtle.

"So you understand the story better. Amy was captain on the same varsity cheerleading squad my sister Beth is on at Alamo Heights."

"Were you ever a cheerleader?"

"No, but I'm glad I never was. I have horrible coordination."

"Interesting. It seemed too feminine for me…if that makes any sense," replied Myrtle as she looked at her freshly painted nails.

"I totally get that."

"So what made Stacy take her daughter from school?"

"Stacy left work early to go shopping at Nieman Marcus last week. She was moving into the dressing room when she recognized someone from the squad fixing her skirt by the mirror. The girl panicked as she stopped to say hello just as her husband came out of the room still buttoning his pants."

"Oh that poor woman. I can't imagine what she felt," said Myrtle.

"Sometimes you never really know who people are."

"Did your sister say what Stacy did?"

"Stacy slapped him and asked how he could put self-interests before their family. She then told the girl that she would be calling her mother as the girl begged for her not to say anything, but Stacy told her to get back to school."

"Parents have to do some pretty tough stuff sometimes," said Myrtle coolly. "It comes with the territory."

"Funny you say that because I thought the same thing."

"Did Amy mention how her mother told her about her father?"

"My sister says when Amy got home, her mother was burning her father's clothes in the brick oven on the deck. She didn't even have time to ask what was happening when Stacy told her to get into the car."

"Oh my. You can't get more manic than that."

"Apparently Stacy never told her who the girl was, but when she told her what her father had done the following day, Amy was devastated because she felt her father took her away from her friends."

"Where did they go?"

"San Francisco."

"How tasteless of that man to expose that girl to such things. How demoralizing," said Myrtle.

"Men have their own set of principles."

"That's true. But he was married. I'm not surprised the mother did what she did."

"I agree. But my sister thinks she overreacted."

"I can see that. But can I ask what you would've done?"

"I wouldn't only because I'm already dealing with so much right now."

"You're a bright girl, so I'll put it to you this way. When a man or woman no longer wants anything to do with their family. Is there anything left to preserve once self-interest becomes the motive? It's obvious the mother wanted to remove her daughter from that predatory environment."

"I see your point."

Melissa had a genuine heartache for the story, but it made her recall a deep-seated memory about her ex-boyfriend. It had been one year today that he disbanded after learning about the pregnancy. She had no intent to get pregnant because she was finishing her bachelor's on loans while her mother battled cancer. It didn't help when Melissa learned two days after her mother's diagnosis that he'd been seeing someone else for the past year. With another year left of college, her sister moved in because their mother's medical costs were quickly rising, leaving her no choice but to get an abortion.

There had been a time she wanted to tell Myrtle because she respected her, and read her magazine religiously. It didn't surprise her to learn about Myrtle's pro-life stance because over the past year Melissa began to see how peoples' views were becoming cynical and hyper-conservative. Since the magazine condemned the pro-choice movement as murders, Melissa decided not to reveal her secret for the fear of losing Myrtle's respect.

Myrtle stood up and paused at the door.

"Melissa, I'll see you next week. Take care."

"You too."

On the way home, Myrtle and Josh gave thanks for the gifts they gave one another. They thought of their children and wanted to praise them since they never caused them trouble. They felt the time they invested in them was paying off.

It was time for church and soon their boys would be in their company. The Collinses had a deep Christian faith they felt rewarded their devotions. Josh in particular felt his success stemmed from that; therefore, he never compromised his conservative views.

♌

Everyone arrived home from Ruth's Chris Steak House, and Myrtle wanted cappuccinos with hazelnut biscottis—so she quickly made them in the kitchen.

Cinnamon was dashed over the crème de la crème before everyone was handed a red cup and saucer. They entered the dining room, where fresh sunflowers sat in a large cerulean vase at the table.

Myrtle dressed her biscotti with foam.

"So, Nathan, now that you're a sophomore. What classes will you be taking next semester?"

Nathan had green eyes with ashy blond hair tossed in all directions. He placed his cup down and wiped his mouth with a blue napkin.

"I plan to take world religions, neo-classical to present-day literature, ethics, creative writing, and philosophy in literature. I'm excited because the writing and neo-classical courses are being taught by a professor who attended Oxford. People say great things about his technique."

Josh lifted an eyebrow. "I remember when I took philosophy as an elective. By the end of the semester, I was miserable. To this day I can't understand why anyone would want a doctorate in philosophy," said Josh.

"I remember tutoring you that semester before you started law school. You clashed with the professor about everything in that class," said Myrtle with a lifted pinky as she took her cup.

"It was bogus."

"Philosophy helps make sense of the corruptness in the world. I can't image the world without it," replied Nathan.

"It should be taught in high school. That way kids would learn common sense at a younger age," added Gregory.

"Do you honestly think a professor would want a high school salary teaching kids common sense when their parents don't have any? Secondly, how can you reach someone when their lives are wrapped up with celebrity gossip and social media?" chuckled Nathan.

"Your father and I remember when education used to be like that. Strict and meaningful. Now parents have to put their kids in private school because public schools don't teach anything anymore," added Myrtle.

"You and Dad went to Alamo Heights, and you did fine," said Gregory.

"Yes. But that's when teachers weren't scared of their students. You could teach with discipline because parents expected it. But more importantly, students appreciated the expectations teachers demanded from them," said Josh.

"If schools didn't lack so many resources. We wouldn't have put you in private school. But people are entitled to protect their interests," added Myrtle.

"I can't believe you said that. You also sound like that woman from Cornell," replied Nathan.

Myrtle grew perky and widened her eyes with interest.

"You mean Ann Coulter?"

"Yes," said Nathan.

"Just because your mother and I went to school with her doesn't mean we follow her religiously. But you have to admit she debates subjects many are scared to bring up," said Josh.

"She spreads garbage," added Gregory.

"Hold on there," said Myrtle clearing her throat. "Her message isn't all that controversial as people make it out to be. I was a sophomore studying communications when she and your father were seniors. She was an idol to a lot of girls because she helped establish the *Cornell Review.*"

"I don't buy that. Anyone who's outspokenly racist has self-esteem issues," replied Nathan.

"That's not an argument," said Josh.

"Course it is."

"Why? Because she's against the separation of church and state?" said Myrtle.

"No. Because she thinks liberals support lazy, overpaid public school teachers responsible for Americans' intellectual decline. Yet everyone knows the country's future rests on the education system. If you keep undermining it, then you'll really run into problems," said Nathan.

"Like I said. We don't follow her religiously. Weren't you paying attention?"

"Well, Dad, he has a point. In history class we debate about her sometimes, and one of the questions that comes up is how she purposefully mispresents facts. What's scary about that is that she's preaching to the choir," said Gregory.

"Really? What *facts* are you referring to?" asked Myrtle.

"That Muslims are a danger to the world. George Bush was right to invade Iraq. Killing Saddam Hussein. That liberals support terrorism."

"Well, honey. If you want to sell books, you need a platform to sell to," replied Myrtle.

Gregory laughed and finished the last of his cappuccino.

"If that's your argument. How will publishing stay legit with alternative facts getting published? It sounds too Goebbels-like if you ask me."

Josh rested his arms on the chair.

"I wouldn't go that far, but I can see why people think she's the devil," said Josh as he took his cup. "Regardless of your views. I want you boys to know how proud we are of you. Because when we're gone, we can rest knowing your brotherly love will nurture one another no matter the obstacle."

"Yeah. Well when that happens. We're going back east where you should've stayed," said Gregory.

"Your Father and I thought about living in Rochester, Syracuse or Ithaca. But the winters are too longer there. So we came back home," said Josh.

"You could've considered San Francisco or Los Angeles if you wanted something warmer. But you've always liked that small-town vibe," added Nathan.

"It's where we wanted to raise a family. Not in some city where people throw attitude for no reason," replied Myrtle.

"I still think you should've stayed somewhere back east," said Gregory.

"When the two of you finish college. You can live wherever you like," added Josh.

Myrtle sat back to admire how her sons were maturing gracefully. She felt few families had the determination to raise a proper family anymore.

She thought about her childhood and remembered that work and leisure had to be equal. Her parents taught her early on that mannerisms must be in check because people based your intelligence on them.

When they finished talking, Josh offered his hand in hers and saw a fearless woman. He still saw the young girl he met when they were young, but now that those chapters had passed, he wouldn't go back because he was enjoying his stability.

Gregory stood up and collected the dishes as they bid each other good night. The boys finished washing the dishes before they turned out the lights and moved to their bedrooms. Moonlight streamed through the skylights and soon the house was fast asleep.

V

IRONY

Wednesday, May 7, 2008: 5.00 p.m.

Puddles squished beneath me as the rain cascaded the umbrella. I entered the building and the flight of stairs fumed with mildew. The soggy blue carpet in the green lit hall was littered with imprints.

Smoke oppressed the joint of familiar faces that catered to doctors, lawyers, and business executives. The ambiance was dim, but it was still noticeable when someone looked at you.

Ben, the bartender, had a gracious personality. His green eyes danced against the red lights over the bar. The enamel paint over the counter was smooth and black.

"Haven't seen you in a while. How you been?" he asked.

My shoes began to chill in the cold room.

"I've been good. How about you?"

"My girlfriend moved out last week."

"Sorry to hear that."

"I'm not. Ever since rent shot up a hundred bucks three days ago. I asked her to pitch in. She said no, so I asked her to move out."

"I would've done the same thing if it wasn't serious."

"It wasn't. I know better than to take pussy over money."

"Any friends open to the idea of sharing a one-bedroom?"

"Can't think of any. I put an ad on Craigslist, though."

"Too many loonies to do that, buddy."

Ben held two thumbs up with a grin. His thick beard didn't hide his boney face, which carried a contempt that was satisfying to look at. The flannel shirt contoured his lanky body as he rested his palms on the counter. It was impossible to not notice his short blond and shiny curly hair.

"After the last girl. There isn't a *looney* I couldn't handle."

"Aside from that. Has anything else happened?"

"My uncle died last month because he couldn't afford his seizer medication."

"I'm sorry to hear that. Were you close?"

"We were, but I wasn't surprised when my sister found him two days later after he'd fallen down the stairs during an episode."

The image of a lifeless body flashed in my mind.

"Was she his caretaker?"

"Not full-time. But we couldn't believe he didn't say anything about his premiums fluctuating."

"Well—like I tell everyone. It's getting rough out there. We all need to hang in there."

Pain burned from his green eyes when he saw that I was truly listening. I admired those who pushed on without letting life shackle them.

It was four in the afternoon and the room was growing louder. It signified that my meeting was around the corner.

"You here by yourself?" he asked.

"My business partner asked me to meet him here—"

A woman suddenly approached the bar with eyes that flared unforgivingly. She was ghostly white with impeccable straight red hair.

"Give me another Chopin on the rocks," she said brashly.

"Right away,"

She sucked on a cigarette before a stream of smoke escaped her lips.

"Here you are, Mrs. Smith. Did you want to close out?"

Her slender fingers clasped the glass, and in two gulps the liquid vanished. Another drag was inhaled coolly with annoyance.

"Hit me again."

"Some day, huh?" I added delicately.

Her raspy voice was icy. "You can't save everyone."

"How do you mean?"

"Bodies don't fight like they used to. Illness is taking everyone so unexpectedly…the numbers are coiling."

"Are you a general practitioner?"

"I practice internal medicine."

The drink was placed on the napkin, but this time it was savored with a sip.

"You must see all sorts of ailments."

"People didn't always demand drugs with more side effects than benefit. But these days everything's backwards."

"Why is that surprising?"

"It's not," gulping her drink before waving at Ben. "One more. Then close me out."

"I have a friend who works at Methodist hospital. His stories can be alarming that I'm glad I'm not in the medical field," I said.

"In twenty-five years when all the baby boomers start retiring. The days will be nothing but malpractice, shortage of nurses, and infinite hours."

"Aren't hours good for your field?"

"People think the industry is easy money, so they get into the field. But once they experience the work. They change careers."

"Is there really a shortage of nurses?"

"Shortage!" she added with a cackle. "Talk about scarcity. Young nurses have no idea the type of hard work that's coming their way. Once the general public sees what the baby boomers are about to experience. People aren't gonna want to live past sixty."

"That doesn't sound very encouraging," I said.

"What do you expect? The experienced nurses, which are the baby boomers, won't be available to mentor the younger nurses once they retire."

"I never thought about that."

"Now would be a good time, because those retirees are worried about the care they're going to receive since the experience will soon be obsolete. You and I will be in that same boat one day."

"I don't know how you do it. I wouldn't have the stamina for that kind of insanity."

"You do what has to be done."

"Do patients drive you crazy?"

"You get accustomed to it. They all ask for meds for imaginary symptoms. People who expect pills to mask apathy so they can wallow in their destructive lifestyles," she said.

"I imagine you refuse that behavior a lot."

"Well, when you have people say 'I pay good money for my insurance—so give me my money's worth. I'm not on Medicaid.' You sort of oblige. I offer diet and exercise routines. But they just want pills."

Her personality was compelling.

"So how do you feel about class action suits?"

"Malpractice suits and liability premiums cause a lot of doctors to retire early or go out of business because malpractice insurance is astronomical. It's the reason doctors run so many unnecessary tests when they find out a patient has insurance. They're constantly covering their ass."

"Better to be safe than sorry, right?" I said.

"Depends. A doctor can have a patient's interests at heart 100 percent. But for whatever reason a test is missed and a diagnosis leads to complications that could've been avoided had additional tests been done. A suit is filed."

"Yeah, but doesn't that unnecessary testing raise the insurance premiums for everyone else?"

"Yes. That's why so many people don't like Medicaid. Sure, some doctors opt out from helping the forty-eight million people on Medicaid. But for those that do. That's a lot of tests being run on the backs of taxpayers already paying pricy private insurance costs."

"I bet the capping law in 2003 helped with that," I said.

"It did. But I can still feel like a physician without rights. Some doctors have sold their practice to work in hospitals thinking the stress will lessen. But big business is everywhere these days."

"I like how you can admit that."

Reluctance stirred in her gaze as I wondered whether she thought she shouldn't have told me the things she did.

She leaned forward and said, "My name is Alley Michaels."

"Nice to meet you, Alley. I'm Christian Wall."

"I was so busy talking my head off I never asked about you."

"No worries, your story was interesting."

"Thank you."

"Like yourself—my life also involves clients."

"You a lawyer?"

I laughed jovially.

"I'm on the Bar Association of the Fifth Federal Circuit."

"What areas you practice?"

"I represent plaintiffs, defendants, corporations, and complex business disputes."

Her hand went into her white Dior leather purse.

"It's never a bad idea to have a litigator on hand. Here's my card in case you ever need a favor."

"I didn't know doctors carried business cards."

Scarlet burned at her cheeks when she saw that I noticed her diamond wedding band. It was obvious the exchange was professional.

"Here's mine. You know—just in case," I said with a smile.

She stood up and put on her red raincoat over a white sweater. Her blue heels graveled the floor until she left.

Josh appeared from the darkness and moved toward me. A blue tie rested impeccably against his white oxford and gray pants. He was always meticulous about his looks, but his sternness proved his heterosexuality.

He was in his early forties and his practice had represented an impressive roaster of clients both in jury and non-jury settings. His experience ranged from civil claims involving contracts, partnerships, real estate, fiduciary duties, deceptive trade practices, employment, insurance, sexual torts, administrative issues, and complex divorces. Many of the cases had been argued in appeals courts in the Fifth and Eleventh Circuits.

"Sorry I'm late. Last-minute work as usual," he said.

"Tell me about it."

"Who was that?"

"Just someone to kill time with."

"Did you get her number?"

I handed him the card and called Ben over.

"So Alley's an internal medicine specialist. Nothing like a sexy woman with brains."

Josh didn't know about my sexual preference. All he knew was that Miranda and I had divorced due to irreconcilable differences. Others had pestered me to make myself available again, but having gone through an expensive divorce was *the* reason I could hide behind.

It was easy to stay private since my firm only had two secretaries and two litigation assistants. Had I worked at Josh's firm, his three administrative assistants, two litigation attorneys, paralegals, and runners would've made things difficult. Only a handful of friends knew about me, but that was more than enough.

"I know. Was just seeing if she was a possible match," I said.

"I was wondering when you were going to start dating again."

"One step at a time."

Ben leaned against the bar and said, "What can I get you fellas?"

"The usual," said Josh with an air.

"The only time we discuss work is when we're not at work. So what do you have for me?" I said.

The drinks were placed on the counter as Josh placed the black briefcase on his lap and handed me a pamphlet.

Josh placed the briefcase on his lap and opened a pamphlet.

"Derek at the attorneys' Western District Office forwarded this to me. Thought you would find it interesting—"

The letter went as follows:

A veteran by the name of Kate, eighteen years of age, had been in the Special Forces for a month when she was raped by a brigade of solders in Iraq. After reporting the incident, she was transferred to another division. Multiple samples of semen were retrieved from her vagina. This is one of many lawsuits being filed against to the Pentagon's defense secretaries Donald Rumsfeld and Robert Gates for failing to prosecute the offenders, and for retaliating against the men and women for reporting the sexual assaults.

The document receded back into the briefcase.

"Interesting, I know. But that isn't why we're here. I wanted to ask if you wanted to take on some appeals for me," said Josh.

"How many?"

"Ten."

"Why don't you want them?"

"I have enough work right now. Besides, you have child support."

"Fair enough."

The bartender approached us and asked, "Another round?"

"Sure. But put Josh's tab with mine."

At the opposite end of the bar a roar of men's laughter contaminated the room.

Josh swigged at the seventeen-year-old Balvenie and replied snobbishly, "Bloody amateurs."

"You know them?"

"You see that guy with the light blue shirt?"

"Yeah."

"He specializes in family litigation. He just won a case against one of the top aviation attorneys in the state."

"What was the dispute over?"

"A helicopter. His client wanted it, so she got to keep it while her husband ended up dishing out five million in damages. His contingent fee was twenty-five percent, so you can imagine he's pretty happy right now."

"Sounds like a win to me."

"Not really."

"But didn't you just—"

"I know what I told you," said Josh brashly. "But how can you be a winner when you enjoy shoving money up your ass?"

Josh was known for speaking his mind, but he wasn't the only one to shame people publicly. But I was accustomed to working with arrogant bigots that playing along was easy.

"I take it you'll never work with him," I said.

"Are you kidding?" as Josh brought the glass to his lips. "The fag attempted to hire me for a case six months ago. But I made sure he wouldn't try that again."

"I bet you did."

"Do you blame me?"

"No."

"Well now that you know. You can avoid him if he tried contacting you."

"Is he from the area?"

"Someone like that wouldn't be."

"I'm not following?" I said.

"Of course you don't," as he took a sip of scotch. "I wouldn't expect you to know about his repulsive arrangement he has going on. But he's a transplant from Houston."

"What arrangement are you talking about?"

"His partner is a man who woke up one day with the idea that he was a woman trapped in a man's body."

"A transgender."

"Yeah. One of those. Well apparently his partner's already imploded his dick and acquired tits. Not sure what to make of that."

"And how do you know this?"

"I know everything in this town."

"I'll give you that. But as long as the couple's happy. I don't see how the altercation harms anyone."

"What gives them a bad name more than anything is how they force laws on people."

"Like what?"

"Well. Just because a man hates his cock doesn't mean they have the right to use the woman's bathroom."

Shocked by the comment. I slowly finished my drink, closed the tab, and put on my blazer.

"I hate to cut things short. But I have some last-minute errands to finish. I better get a move on."

"Thanks for taking the favor," Josh added.

"No problem."

I descended the mildew-fumed staircase and stepped outside. As I moved down the sidewalk, the rain spilled over the umbrella.

VI

Television

Tuesday, May 20, 2008: 9.00 p.m.

Gregory receded from the restroom with moisture on his skin. He saw a smooth, ripped chest and torso in the mirror. He was satisfied with his body and he enjoyed the attention whether he was clothed or at swim practice. His cock was still erect from having just masturbated. He squeezed the last bit of semen from the tip and licked his finger.

The telephone rang on the nightstand.

"Hello?"

Jeanie was on the bed with her physics textbook. The lamp was covered with a red cloth and the ambiance distorted the walls. A television sat on a black console where her stereo and books were tightly packed. Her provocative voice trickled through the earpiece. "I'm not ready for school tomorrow."

He recognized the tone in her voice "Why the frustration?"

Gregory placed jojoba in his palm and spread it over his body.

"They need to stop cramming projects, tests, and finals all in one day," she said.

Gregory could hear the CNN headlines through the earpiece: *Pentagon has announced that a deployment of 42,000 troops, including 25,000 active Army soldiers, will be sent to Iraq beginning in the fall to replace troops returning home by year's end.*

"What else would there be to do?" Gregory asked.

Jeanie ignored the comment because as much as she loved him, he had ways of irritating her.

"I'm ready for summer vacation. It's been a year from hell."

"Every year is hell for you."

She rolled her eyes with flout.

"I have to work harder at this than you do."

"Bullshit. Being in the top six takes more than just turning in homework."

This made her smile. There was nothing they didn't tell one another because their vulnerability for truth was very fragile.

"You can say the sweetest things sometimes," she said with a sigh.

"I know you study a lot. But at least you're getting somewhere."

She moved to her desk and pulled an assortment of papers from a binder.

"I know."

"Any plans for summer?" Gregory asked.

"Not yet, but something will come up."

"You sound funny. Something on your mind?"

"My art portfolio is going to be counted twice. So it needs to be flawless," she replied genially.

"Don't sweat it. You're the best in our class."

Jeanie blushed because she knew it was true, but the reassurance helped.

"I didn't tell you what happened at the store today," she said.

"Another guy gave you his number."

"Stop it! I'm being serious."

"All right. What happened?"

Jeanie began shading a picture of a skull over her book cover.

"We were about to check out when my mom asked if I needed anything else. As usual, I forgot to get my late July chocolate cookies, so I dashed to get them. Before I took the box, a little girl, no older than eight, was pointing at a woman. It was one of those instances when you don't know what's happening until you're forced to. So when the girl said loudly, 'Look, Mommy, she must be rich!' Everyone in the aisle tried not to look at the child, but when I did, so did everyone else. The mother slapped the child and yelled, 'Lucy. That's unacceptable!' before they stormed away."

Gregory chuckled because he thought childhood was more formative than adolescence.

He wasn't surprised because he thought society was too impetuous. He felt children needed more discipline so they could learn not to be obnoxious later in life. Gregory knew he was a teenager, but since his parents were strict; his personality was refined.

"What was in the lady's basket?" he asked.

"Brand-named foods."

"And the woman who slapped the child?"

"Store-brand foods."

Gregory closed the restroom door and slid into bed.

"If *you* were having financial troubles I'm sure you wouldn't want people knowing. Especially strangers."

Jeanie felt defensive.

"True. But the mother didn't need to slap the kid."

"How old do you think she was?"

"Around ten."

"She was old enough to know not to say things like that."

The headlines flashed: *Pastor John Hagee said during a sermon that Nazis operated on*

God's behalf to chase the Jews from Europe.
Catches campaign trail by surprise.

Jeanie thrashed her hair in the air and shrieked with annoyance.

"My debate in Mr. Hickson's class at the end of the week is making me anxious because I'm ready to blow Chelsi's ass in the dirt."

"Poor thing doesn't stand a chance."

"When I saw our names on the roster, I knew it was too good to be true."

"Speaking of debate. Mine's on Friday."

"Who's your opponent?"

"George."

Gregory knew they could talk about anyone without judgment. Between them, Gregory felt he was more modest because when they were together. Strangers could sense Jeanie's elitism more than his.

"You mean, speedy George," she said.

"Yes."

"I'm sure he'll be doped as usual."

A sigh of annoyance was expressed.

"What do you have against him?"

"He tried selling to me."

"You never told me that."

"It wasn't relevant enough to."

"When did this happen?"

"I was in the library studying for a chemistry exam last month when a shadow loomed over me. His eyes were deranged as he lethargically moved. He had no problem asking, 'Ever have any fun besides books? I have something I think you might like,' as a sheet of foil was removed from his pocket."

"The poor guy was frying on acid."

"He's fortunate he came to me because if he went to the wrong person. They would've ratted on him."

"Why didn't you?"

"I don't hate him enough to get him expelled."

"So what did you say?"

"Nothing. He just zoned out and straggled away."

"Bizarre."

The headline flashed: *Senator Edward Kennedy diagnosed with brain cancer—three days after seizure.*

"I can't believe the faculty hasn't gotten him expelled. I mean, how he passes his coursework is amazing."

"You should've asked him."

"Gregory! You know what I mean."

There was a knock at the door.

"Come in," Gregory answered.

Myrtle appeared under the archway in a white silk gown. The smell of fresh nail polish tickled his nose.

"Am I interrupting anything?" Myrtle asked.

"It's only Jeanine."

"What's that supposed to mean?" as she rolled her eyes. "She should be glad it's me."

Myrtle was fond of her because she was a good influence on Gregory. They never got into trouble and Myrtle felt confident that Jeanie's mother cared about her daughter's future.

"I have an important meeting tomorrow morning. So I won't have time to make breakfast. Be sure to wake up early so you can stop somewhere before class."

"Okay. Don't be too hard on them tomorrow."

She walked in and kissed his forehead.

"Then nothing would get done. You know I couldn't allow that."

Jeanie removed her bra and looked at her breasts in the mirror. She recalled the rumors last year of how she let the track team fuck her in the ass, but it wasn't true. The only thing that concerned her was whether the rumors proved that she was sexually desirable. But what she truly wanted to know was if people perceived her as beautiful.

"Did I tell you I started writing again?" she said.

"I thought you gave that up?"

"So did I. But the stress this week rekindled the drive."

"I wished writing helped my frustrations like they did yours."

"It's the lesser of evils."

"I doubt that."

She crawled into bed.

"Really. So *passion doesn't* drive people to do crazy things?"

"Is that the kind of motivation you want?"

"Naturally."

"That wasn't an answer."

Jeanie could feel the anger in her thoughts. Though she was too young to know what true anger was, she knew passion created her focus.

"I'm tired of fundamentalists trying to fulfill biblical Armageddon," as she switched off the TV and turned on her stereo to play "Muscoviet Musquito."

She had her ideologies, but the irony was that they were attainable. The only barrier was that people believed too much in apathy's promises, and that irritated her.

He closed his eyes and wondered what it would be like to see the flash and feel the radiation melt his flesh over his disintegrating bones.

"In a sick way—destruction is seductive," replied Gregory.

"That's a sign that death truly walks amongst the living."

She sighed and imaged what it would be like to be like everyone else. But to give up her ideas was worse than treachery. Because if there was no one left to question the world with introspection. Reason would dissolve from hope. "If it's any consolation, Jeanine. People will eventually come to their senses, but first they have to recede from the darkness."

"Being voiceless is a crime, Gregory. Can you imagine a world where people accept that? Not out of force—but because they chose to?"

"That's already happened."

"So is life only capable of existing in pain?"

"Yes. Because if life was perfect. There wouldn't be conflict to stir creativity."

The night consumed their thoughts as they wondered how others questioned the same trivialness.

"Sometimes I feel like I'm trapped in Pier Pasolini's *Salò*," replied Jeanie.

"No wonder you're gloomy. Have you watched it recently?"

"Yes. His message intrigues me."

"How so?"

"Both you and I know how shady it was that he was murdered before *Salò* was released."

"Yeah. The film was a middle finger to Italian fascists, political corruption, sadism, consumerism, and perversion."

"Ironically, he was fortunate to live through the Years of Lead. A lot was going on politically and he was able to capture that in his films and writing."

"Ever since the case reopened in 2005. Authorities thought the new developments would solve the case."

"But they didn't," said Jeanie dryly.

"I know. But, in 1975 many questioned Pelosi's original story because he was too frail to inflict Pasolini with multiple broken bones, crushed testicles, and a partially burned body. The DNA taken from Pelosi's clothes proved it belonged to at least three people. It shows he couldn't have acted alone despite him confessing he worked alone."

"But people already knew neo-fascists murdered him because his views and homosexuality threatened the Cristian-Democratic establishment."

"*Salò* used to scare me, but now it resembles a warning. How dark things can get when you surrender to materialism and immediate gratification without listening to the consequences."

"I agree."

Jeanie rolled over and set her alarm.

"Listen. It's getting late and we have a lot to do this week."

Gregory switched off the television and watched the trees swaying outside the window.

"I'll see you in third period."

"Good night, Gregory."

He lay in bed and listened to the silence. He thought about the man he met and became aroused. Their first night together was everything Gregory hoped it would be. The rebellion felt natural and the rush was becoming addicting.

Christian made him feel at peace for having brought him to the bridge that crossed the void that had been growing. He used to question himself, but the more he learned about the world, he trusted his instincts.

Once he was asleep, he dreamt of a blue sea that stretched into the horizon. Seagulls circled in a cloudless sky as the sail flapped in the wind.

Gregory was resting on my lap, and his eyes sparked against the sun. His palm touched my face with affection.

"What's on your mind?" I asked.

The only sound was the water splashing along the boat's side. And far off in the distance a red buoy silently swayed.

"I had a peculiar dream the other night. It was horrible," Gregory said.

"What happened?"

"Somehow I was left in the dark shouting for you to rescue me—but you never came."

I continued to run my fingers through his hair.

"It was only a nightmare. There's nothing to worry about. Nothing like that will happen as long as I'm here. I promise," I said.

"I hope so. Because right now I feel like we're the luckiest people alive."

"Just know if anything happened. I would dive into the abyss to find you. Even if all the treasure in the world was found—I would give it up to have you."

Gregory smiled and said, "I know you would."

VII

TWILIGHT

Saturday, September 13, 2008: 8.00 p.m.

The full moon followed Gregory and I along the highway as "Dreams Never End" blared from the stereo. There was no denying the charge as our hands rested on the stick shift. He wore light blue slim-fit trousers with a collared pink shirt. His slicked hair accentuated his seductiveness as the cologne filled the cabin.

He wasn't seen as a conquest, but rather an individual whose confidence created an unspeakable lure. In the beginning I doubted the

relationship because guys were never serious
about anything but sex, but that changed.

When we arrived at the restaurant, the foyer
smelled of anise. The dim room was coated in red
and yellow themes as we moved to the podium.

The chandelier sparkled over the hostess in
a tight black suit. Her hazel eyes present in the
darkness.

"Welcome to Paesanos. How many in your
party?"

"Just two," I said.

The flimsy woman placed the menus at her
bosom.

"Right this way."

We embarked into a room drenched with
lemon zest and butter. Chatter and laughter
blended with shadows chewing their dinner. They
stared from the darkness, but it was impossible to
read their thoughts.

If someone recognized us, Gregory said we
could say I was an advisor from Columbia.

The woman's yellow heels paused at a table
with black cloth.

"Here we are, gentlemen."

We rooted ourselves in green leather booths before being assigned the menus.

"Your server will be with you shortly."

The atmosphere created a mood that was gothic with enchantment. Submersed in noir—it was comical to see how everyone treated the joint as if it were the only place in town.

A young man appeared before us. His blue eyes were clear and his red hair was mashed against his head. His athletic build was worth more than his uniform, but if Gregory knew that, how would it affect his self-esteem?

"My name is Alosha and I'll be serving you this evening," as he opened royal-blue napkins to place on our laps. "What can I get you to drink?"

"We'll take Apollinaris and the house appetizer," I said.

"Excellent choice."

Gregory looked at the orange light above us.

"Amazing how a piece of wallpaper can be decorative."

"Pretty ingenious stuff."

"I hope I get a streak of that someday."

"It's not a question of if—but when."

"You think so?"

"Why not."

His characteristics were fascinating for a young man. If he was clever now—I imagined how he would be a few years from now.

We opened the menus.

"I'm in the mood for a grass-fed lame steak, asparagus, and sautéed spinach," he said.

The waiter produced the refreshment with a plate of celery sticks and goat cheese. He poured the elixir into the glasses and garnished them with mint.

We had been ready to order, so when the server asked, "How would you like that cooked?" Gregory answered, "Bloody."

He nodded with assurance and dropped the notepad in his apron.

There had been a group of women engaged in a lively conversation behind us. The subject became apparent when one of the women said, "—the twenty-four karat diamond is from Tiffanies. —Are you kidding? I wouldn't accept anything less. —How he paid for it. Who cares? —Just as long as it looks fabulous on me."

The woman got up and left to the restroom. She was in a black open-shoulder blouse with black pants. When she came back, it was strange how her face had been slathered with makeup. Her neck, arms, and hands were much darker with obvious signs that she was a smoker. Her frame was thin with dry skin.

Gregory reached for the celery and dressed it with cheese.

"Have you noticed that people treat food like social etiquette?" he said.

"How do you mean?"

"Well…people eat certain foods around certain people. As if they're being monitored in a controlled experiment."

"Some have the need to impress others— even if it's ridicules. Snobbery mustn't be mistaken for personal preference."

Gregory wrinkled his brow.

"Interesting how people make a great survival guide," he added.

"The sooner you master leaving your plate half full, the faster you'll blend into society. Always remember when someone decides to be uncouth or wasteful. It doesn't mean they're a dupe."

Our dinner arrived with a train of servers to embellish our table. Gregory's point about our privileged life manifested because it was going to be impossible to finish the meal. And that somehow left me spiteful. The thought didn't last long because I wasn't trying to flash money, but spend time with Gregory.

"Is there anything more I can get you gentlemen?"

"Not right now. Thank you," I said.

Gregory took the silverware and sliced the steak.

"This may be odd. But have you ever wondered why agitation is strongest at night?"

"Is something bothering you?"

"Sort of."

"Are your parents agitating you again?"

"Yes."

"Are you doing anything to stay occupied?"

"I've been writing in my journal."

"Good things, I hope."

"Well—"

"I was only joking. I know you're using it to vent. But it's funny you mentioned that because I used to have a journal when I was in school. I used to imagine the ink were parts of my soul that would never come back. It was comforting."

"Do you still have it?"

"I got rid of it. Memories can create negative energy sometimes."

We took a moment to savor the meal.

"I like writing at night because it clears my head."

"A lot of people would agree with that. What did you focus on?"

"I promised myself to experience more sacrifice."

The waiter appeared at our table.

"Would you gentlemen care for any dessert?"

We agreed that espresso sounded appetizing.

"That's an interesting thought. What made you feel like that?" I said.

"I suppose perception did."

"There has to be more to it than that."

"People are just more sensitive to their emotions than others. For example, physiatrists that dope their patients instead of counseling them—isn't an answer. Most of the time mental-static can be stabilized, but medicine only goes so far compared to holistic methods."

"I agree. It's usually artists who are hyper-sensitive to the environment. Which explains why the best are usually ill or temperamental," I said.

"Complexity has never been tolerated in our society."

"I advise caution with that because a drop of water never admits its involvement in a flood."

"You should tell my parents that."

The clatter of silverware clinked in the background. The crowd had thinned, but the room was still busy. The espresso arrived in turquoise cups and Gregory reclined in the booth.

I savored a sip of the crème de la crème and said, "The smart ones go against the norm—they refuse to be ignorant."

Gregory took the cup and finished the drink.

"That explains why pharmaceutical companies want our emotions altered. So they can brainwash us into thinking our emotions are the enemy," he said.

The waiter took our cups and left us with a cheerful farewell.

"Every day is a learning experience. Even if you end up at the same spot from where you began. Tenacity always wins."

I opened the leather booklet and signed the receipt. We moved through the room to the foyer.

The hostess opened the door and replied, "Have a lovely evening."

VIII

MELANCHOLY

Saturday, September 14, 2008: 12.00 a.m.

I wanted to admit that Gregory was too young, but the more I reflected how I was at his age. It was justified. His flair for life was moving, and our energy was in sync. It was exciting dropping him off at home after dinner while I waited thirty minutes for him to sneak back out. There was no question he could've been caught, but he was relying on the obliviousness of his parents to take advantage of the situation.

When we got to my place, he excused himself to the restroom and I sat down to think about when I was in college.

I never feared about others finding out about me, but when my roommate's girlfriend found her fiancé's legs around my shoulders one night, she told everyone on campus. Greg was so embarrassed—he left to Yale the following semester. There was a lot of friction after that, but it didn't stop me from finishing law school at Columbia.

I questioned whether being first in my class had anything to do with their animosity or if being gay was the reason. I imagined if they thought a homosexual couldn't beat them, but she got her revenge when her parents told my family since they knew them well. By the time I graduated with honors, my grandparents forgot the fiasco.

But the revenge didn't stop there. During my last semester I was called into the dean's office because someone accused me of cheating during finals. After I was almost expelled, the office received an anonymous letter stating I hadn't cheated—exposing the pupil responsible for the lie. I never found out who it was, but two weeks later Jonathan Knights was expelled for breaking the honor code. Various alumni tried contacting me later to apologize when word got out that Miranda wasn't bitter about the breakup even though we already had Timothy. But I wanted knowing to do with them.

When Gregory came out of the restroom, my thoughts ended.

"Can we go on the terrace?" he asked.

"Sure."

The view painted the sky with a texture that smelt hallow. The moon illuminated the sky as the pillars glowed with industrial splendor.

Gregory moved to the other side of the railing. The wind carried his voice in a cool fashion.

"Can I tell you something?" he said.

I placed my hands in my pockets.

"Sure."

"I've been having strange dreams."

Curiosity consumed me.

"Different or reoccurring ones?"

"Reoccurring."

"Are they worrying you?"

"I think so because they're growing with intensity."

"It takes time to interpret them."

His eyes had nostalgia flowing through them. His thoughts made me recall the darkness youth could carry.

Noise rose from the streets as the wind tasseled his hair. His melancholy demeanor wasn't an issue, but I wondered how someone so young could be so introspective.

His assertiveness was an attribute not found in people unaccustomed with struggle. He recognized his flaws when others denied theirs. His cathartic need to talk about his imperfections was satisfying.

His eyes could retrieve the truth from anyone. But if you had nothing to hide you—they had no effect.

"What if I don't want to?"

"It's unusual for someone not to care why."

"I don't think dying in your dreams is something that shouldn't be taken lightly," he added exhaustingly.

"That shouldn't frighten you."

"Just because I brought it up doesn't mean it does."

"Why did you?"

He gazed from the shore that was miles away.

"I'm concerned because I wake up screaming sometimes."

"All right. What bothers you most when you're awake?"

"Wishing the world didn't care who I cared about."

"So do I."

"After I accepted the fact that I wouldn't be able to change my attraction toward men. There was no one I could talk to about that, so I put myself in denial. I secretly hated myself. I became numb and forgot who I was, but the funny thing about denial is that it can change the scenery—not the emotions."

"I understand how *outside* influence can be overwhelming. But we mustn't let *them* run our lives because they don't know what's best for us."

He smiled.

"I know. But it's hard when you're outnumbered.... Even my closest friends on the swim team make me feel lost. I constantly tell myself, 'Why settle for this?' Yet I persist being someone else."

"Negativity finds those who brood. If you allow that—it becomes you. So if your friends make you feel like that—you need to reevaluate that."

"That's what I admire about you. You actually listen to me. You help make sense out of things I can't trust in others."

A gust of wind grazed between us.

"We seemed to have found something to hold onto. Not everyone takes that risk."

"Once I realized everyone is scared of having their feelings toyed with. I took the chance."

His confession was an open wound craving to be mended. I wanted to be that healing touch so I could forever be the mended scar.

"I can't promise you everything. But as long as we have each other, life can be manageable."

We held one another as if the world were deteriorating.

"I just don't want the hopeless emptiness to come between us," he said.

Hearing that was sinful because even he knew there were no guarantees in life. He was young, therefore he was allowed to be hopeful. My views were usually optimistic, but that didn't mean time had a way of changing things.

IX

RELIEF

Tuesday, November 11, 2008

A candle flame danced on blue walls as Jeanie painted a white rose on her canvas. She was in a studio her parents had built in the backyard. The solitude meant everything to her because her parents always had the television broadcasting when they weren't watching. Her thoughts couldn't flow in the static because it wanted her to forget the value of art.

The phone vibrated in her pocket.

"What's up?" she said.

"What you doing?"

"Painting."

"Anything good?"

"Not really. Just glad Super Tuesday is over."

Her standing desk stood next to a black beanbag. And resting on the gray hardwood floor was a white Darby wool shag rug.

Gregory pictured her tongue between her teeth as she rinsed her brush in the water.

"Too bad the dream ticket never panned out," replied Gregory.

"True. But at least the Bush Administration will be out of the White House and the world can join us in a farewell celebration."

A gust of wind rustled through the trees. Gregory was in his room as moonlight filtered through the windows. Various sketches from art class hung on the wall. His favorite was a decrepit rocking chair resting on a flaking deck.

"Is your brother coming for Christmas break?" Jeanie asked.

"Yeah, but he's going to spend two weeks in Quebec first."

She brushed the last stroke.

"I've always envied his brains. His meticulous personality makes me jealous."

Gregory silently agreed because out of everyone in the family, Nathan had a presence about him. He exuded confidence, but he was equally approachable.

Gregory had never been jealous of Nathan because he admired him more than anyone in the family. He wanted him to know about his orientation, but if he reacted negatively, his parents would find out and that scared him.

Love seemed conditional in the family and that was upsetting. It was supposed to be unbiased, yet that wasn't the case. This made him feel shameful because their child shouldn't be scared to be home.

It was unfair he felt this way, but being he heard derogatory comments about gay people— it didn't help the tension.

He moved from the floor and climbed into bed.

"How are the SAT classes going?" he asked.

"All right."

"How have your scores been?"

"We've only had one practice exam. The second one is next week. I was fifty points short my goal, but I scored a 2300."

"Keep at it. You'll get there."

"The sacrifices we go through before college is ludicrous. Sometimes I ask if it's worth it."

Gregory could hear "Agents of Oblivion" playing in the background.

"I wouldn't take it that far. How else can we prove our worthiness?"

Gregory heard a knock at Jeanie's door.

"Come in," she said.

Her mother's voice was cold as usual.

"Did you finish your laundry like I asked?"

Jeanie placed her hand over the receiver, but Gregory could still hear the conversation.

"Mother. I'm on the phone."

"Young lady, I don't care if you're talking with the Dali Lama! I asked you a question?"

Jeanie's neck tightened.

"Yes, ma'am. The chores are finished."

Her mother arched her eyebrows and stared at her daughter as if she were translucent. The door quickly shut.

Jeanie removed her hand and swallowed the embarrassment.

"Sorry about that. She's been on edge lately."

"You know why?"

"Apparently a patient became so erratic the other day she had to terminate their contract."

"What happened?"

"She'd been counseling this guy for the past year, but he got belligerent."

"Did he threaten her?"

"No. But everything had to do with his boyfriend moving in a year ago."

Gregory was intrigued since he'd never met a gay couple before.

"So what happened?"

"My mother says there's this website called Adam4Adam where people create dating profiles. The patient noticed his partner using the site six months ago after he moved in."

"That's weird."

"My mom says he chose not to confront his partner. She tried to convince him otherwise, but he didn't want to disrupt the energy in their home since the partner was cofounder of a startup."

"Financial convenience can make people burden unusual circumstances."

"That's what my mother said, but eventually she had to prescribe Celexa since denial was making him depressed and uninterested at his job."

"Where did he work?"

"He was the marketing director for the American Heart Association."

"Interesting."

"Not being able to carry the pressure anymore, her client created a profile to spy on his partner, but my mom wouldn't tell me what he found because the content was too explicit."

Gregory found the conversation disturbing because he was hoping to hear something positive. It wasn't the first time hearing that gay relationships functioned differently from straight ones, and he wanted to know more.

"That's sort of gross," he replied.

"I know."

"What else did she tell you?"

"Well after lying about going out of town on a retreat one weekend. He ended up staying at a hotel downtown, to catch him in bed with someone half his age at their home."

"I imagine the fight was horrible."

"How did you know that?"

"Wild guess."

What puzzled Gregory most was that two young successful men couldn't be happy. He thought about the relationship with Christian and how everything was going fine. He enjoyed Christian's grounded reality because it made their situation very real. Despite Gregory's age, he'd read enough books to know when people were being deceptive…and Christian didn't fit that profile.

"So yesterday while she was in session with another client, the patient came to the office and scared the shit out of the receptionist. He was in a heavy sweat screaming that he swallowed the whole bottle of Celexa and wanted to know when the pills were going to make him feel better."

"I'm sure the receptionist has seen stuff like that before."

"My mother said neither of them had. But after they called the ambulance, she transferred his files to another psychiatrist who specialized in suicidal impulsivities."

"What happened to the patient?"

"She told me she really didn't care because once people got too self-destructive during treatment. She loses sympathy."

"That's understandable."

"I agree. But it's confusing how the situation escalated to that. I mean, if you know someone is cheating, and you think it'll pass—that's crazy. I would've told the person to move out once I knew they weren't happy with me sexually."

"I know. At least your mother wasn't hurt during the meltdown."

Rain began to slither down the windowpanes of Gregory's room.

"Is it raining at your house?"

"Yeah, must be that cold front."

Jeanie dimed the chrome fixture at her yellow desk and rested on the pink sofa by the window. She opened the white curtains and pointed her foot in the air. She admired the veins in her foot and thought, *Too bad I wasn't a ballerina. I have beautiful, strong feet.*

She cleared her thoughts and said, "Yeah, the high tomorrow is supposed to be in the forties."

The wind slammed the limbs against the sides of their house as thunder rattled the sky. When it began to pour, she turned off the light and ran across the lawn.

The air in the house was chilly as her mother hollered from the living room, "I thought you were going to spend the night out there."

"Very funny, Mother."

Her father was in a green sweater sitting at the table with a large stack of papers. Every spotlight was on while her mother read in the corner with a blanket over her knees.

"Jeanie, be a sport and bring me a glass of water since you're in the kitchen," said her father.

She rolled her eyes and opened the cupboard.

She handed him the glass and said, "To my favorite father."

He looked at the phone and said, "Let me guess. Gregory."

"Would you rather I be talking with Charles Manson?"

His light brown hair was airy and styled from earlier in the day. He was lean and tall with frameless glasses. His nose was long and thin, but his robust facial structure with bushy eyebrows concealed its size. He was stern, but his vivaciousness overshadowed it.

"Very funny," he said. "Tell him I say hello."

"He says the same. What you working on?"

"Reconfiguring the Chemistry Department's curriculum."

"Making it harder for those who already have ulcers?"

"Not exactly," as he dismissed the sarcasm. "The American Chemical Society expects certain standards. So I'm making sure Admissions is up to date on these changes."

She leaned forward and kissed his forehead.

"All right. I'll let you get back to work."

She walked upstairs, lit a candle, and lay in bed.

"My parents are such goobers. Makes me wonder how I'm going to be at their age."

"You'll probably be just like your mother."

"Gregory! What an awful thing to say."

"I was joking."

"He was in a good mood considering the stress he's been under."

"So he loves the university. More power to him."

"Trinity asked him to be vice president for Academic Affairs. So I'm sure he does. Anyhow—I don't want to change the subject, but did you order the next book for class?" she asked.

"I stopped by Half Price Books today and surprisingly *Crime and Punishment* was available."

"Were there more copies?"

"No."

She sighed loudly.

"I guess I'll order mine through Amazon then."

He began laughing.

"Don't worry. I took care of it."

"I'm confused."

"They had two copies. So I got them both."

He pictured her cheeks blushing with glassy eyes.

"Always on top of everything. I'll give you the money during third period."

"Don't worry about it."

There were times she wished they could be together. Her heart felt they were always connected, but she valued their friendship too much. Gregory yawned and felt a wave of slumber consume him. He could hardly wait to smell the northern air in the morning.

"My eyes are getting heavy," replied Gregory.

She pulled the comforter over her and blew out the candle.

"See you tomorrow."

The receiver was placed in its nock and the alarm was set. He gazed at the tree's shadow upon the wall and watched it sway. He lost track of time and soon the trees were forgotten.

X

WOMB

Thursday, November 20, 2008: 8.30 a.m.

Myrtle wore a sage Lacroix dress with red heels. Her long legs moved sensually with styled hair flat against her cleavage. She stood in front of a group sitting around a white oval table with white chairs. Concentration consumed their faces as they listened to their editor-in-chief.

"Are we ready to begin?" asked Myrtle.

Everyone softly shuffled their papers in the brightly lit room.

A young women with short black hair raised her hand. She had electric black eyes that pierced through blue-framed glasses. Her red nails gave solid contrast against her purple blouse.

"Yes," replied Myrtle.

"We've only written once about the colony collapse disorder with honeybees. Since then, new information has come to light."

"Will you mention cell phones or GMOs?"

The women grew nervous because Myrtle only asked questions when topics interested her.

"No."

"Then what's the argument?"

"Beekeepers lost more revenue than last year, and people are just beginning to learn about their role with rising food costs consumers are experiencing."

"How can we prove the severity of the issue?"

"We'll tell readers about section 7204 (h) (4) in the 2008 Farm Bill, and how it's funding research for a solution to the crisis."

Myrtle told the woman in purple heels to write *bees* on the whiteboard.

A young man in a yellow Alexander McQueen shirt raised his arm. He had red hair and pale skin and was as thin as a rail. His demeanor was carefree with inexperienced eyes that addressed the room.

"What about an article about José Medellín. The Mexican national convicted of raping and killing two American teenage girls?"

"Texas executed him by lethal injection on August 5th. What's so interesting about that?"

"Since the international court's appeal for a stay in execution was denied. Did we violate the international treaty of 1963?"

"If I remember correctly. He confessed to the murders."

"That's correct—"

"Then what's there to discuss?"

"Some people argue that since the US rendered the treaty's validity. Has that made Americans more at risk for getting arrested overseas?"

Medellín was placed on the board.

Another young woman with frizzy brown hair raised her arm.

"How about a story on IndyMac being the fourth largest bank failure in US history. We can talk about whether the government really needs to bail out private corporations like Freddie Mac and Fannie Mae."

"Too dull. If people don't know that in 1982 the Reagan Administration signed the Garn–St. Germain Depository Act to ease savings and loans regulations. It allowed future deregulations to create the subprime housing crisis we're now afflicted with."

The woman turned red as she tried to look unaffected. When Myrtle saw the embarrassment, she magnified it.

"Megan. There's a reason why people come to work."

"I understand. I'm sorry for that."

"You came unprepared last week, and I asked you not come empty-handed again. I know this is your first journalism job. But my expectations were blatant in the interview."

"I know. But—"

"No. We have people starving out there because history continues to be recycled. Why we continue voting for snake oil salesmen is beyond me."

"But I'm not responsible for that."

Myrtle refrained from showing her shock as she sat still.

"Can you tell me what happened in 1876?" asked Myrtle dryly.

"I'm afraid not."

"Rutherford Hayes lost the popular and electoral votes—yet managed to become president because the Electoral College handed him the presidency in exchange for giving the Confederacy back to the South."

"Isn't that what they wanted to begin with?"

Myrtle disregarded the question and continued.

"Slavery's already ended, so why are rural states getting more power during elections when they're not carrying the country financially?"

"Because it's what makes America great."

"Megan. Your performance has been subpar ever since you started. It's no secret that you've been struggling to keep up with everyone. We enjoy your personality, but today would be a good time to see how quick you can be."

"Okay."

Myrtle straightened her posture and refrained from looking at anyone else. Megan felt deflated as the room gawked at her.

"Name a state that uses nonpartisan judicial commissions for districting."

"Iowa."

"What does it mean when voters aren't choosing their representatives, but representatives are choosing their voters? An effect called hyper-partisan gridlock."

"I don't know."

"Gerrymandering."

Myrtle paused and took a deep breath.

"Let's go back to the Electoral College. But this time I'm going to ask the same question differently. So I want an answer."

"All right."

"The inequality of taxation between wealthier and poorer states has been prevalent for decades. Does that mean a state that pays more in federal taxes should receive less benefits per capita, versus another state that pays less in federal taxes but receives more benefits per capita?"

"I don't think rural states should have much say since they aren't pulling their weight. Red states believe that a dollar spent by the government impoverishes them—shifting their tax dollars to welfare queens in cities."

"All right. When should the federal government offer more funding?"

"During emergencies."

"So doesn't that represent institutional corruption? Meaning—it proves that our country supports bribes, payoffs, and table deals for everyday business?"

"Agreeing with that would be unfair to our country."

"In response to your pervious answer. The South has become the main protector of Republican conservatism in the 21st century. Wouldn't you find that odd since Lincoln was the first Republican president?"

"Yes."

"If you agree—you should also know California is our agricultural breadwinner. It has one of the most vibrant economies—and pays more in federal taxes than it receives. The Electoral College was developed so rural states wouldn't be disowned, but two hundred years later it's the *majority* who are now disenfranchised. So unless a new federalism is instilled. The richer and poorer states will cause another Civil War."

"I see your point. I'll be sure to read up on that. This won't happen again."

"That's correct. It won't," as she fiercely scowled at Megan. "Pack your things and find employment elsewhere."

"But—"

"It's either this or I call Security. What will it be?"

The room grew warm as she gathered her things in silence. Her chin quivered as she pushed through the door. Everyone remained silent until a young man in a green scarf raised his hand. He had a surly but intelligent look from experiencing Myrtle's pressure.

"After North Korea dismantled a water-cooling tower used for plutonium extraction at a Yongbyon facility. Why did the

Six-Party Talks allow them to keep spent-fuel rods?"

He wrote *nuclear* threat on the board and sat down.

"From the subjects here. I want *Medellín* to be our cover story. But only from the perspective on whether we've made American citizens more vulnerable overseas."

The phone rang and Myrtle pressed the speaker.

"Yes—"

"Your two o'clock has arrived."

"Thank you. I'll be in my office shortly."

Myrtle Publications was known for thought-provoking articles. It had been five years since its launch and already Advance Publications controlled its national distribution.

Everyone gathered their things.

"Have a good day, everyone. Remember to have your stories on my desk by Monday morning."

XI

NAUSEA

Tuesday, November 11, 2008: 6.00 p.m.

An electrical storm crept from the Northeast with a menacing grayness.

It was late afternoon and Myrtle was relaxing by the fire with the *New York Times*. A fresh cup of organic white tea steamed beside her.

Josh was upstairs while Gregory sat in the windowsill in his room reading Patrick Süskind's *Perfume.*

Thunder rumbled and Myrtle looked out the window as the phone rang. She placed the paper at her side and saw that it was one of her neighbors.

"Hello, Virginia. How are you?"

Virginia Goodsen was raising two boys and a girl who also attended St. Joseph Academy. Her husband, Donald, was a neurosurgeon and Virginia a plastic surgeon. Their friendship was firm because they constantly bounced ideas off one another. It was no secret they competed with each another, but that sort of thing was expected in their social circles.

Her two sons were freshmen while their daughter went to Harvard the same year Nathan was denied admittance. This upset Nathan, but that was shrugged off when the University of Toronto offered a better scholarship.

Virginia and Donald could think themselves superior over the Collinses, but Virginia really liked their family. From day one the Goodsens wanted to live around people who were as accomplished as they were. They were ambitious, but extremely unforgiving toward laziness.

The Collins also had a competitive edge in Alamo Heights, but they weren't quick to live in the largest house in the district. Myrtle and Josh agreed that if they made as much money as the Goodsens, they wouldn't display it so extravagantly. They instilled modesty in their children, but sometimes it looked contradictory since both their children went to one of the most prestigious private schools in the nation. The Collinses could've lived in a modest neighborhood, but they chose not to because they wanted to experience their accomplishments.

"How are you this evening?" Virginia asked.

"Good. How about yourself?"

Virginia opened the white French doors in her bedroom and sat by the window. A roll of thunder passed overhead.

"It's been interesting," she said.

"How so?"

"Well, I was leaving work one day and a panhandler who solicits from his usual spot along the interstate had a new sign that read, 'Are your veterans buried with an American-made flag?' When I got home, I asked Donald to get the flag case from the wall. When I opened it, Donald blurted, 'What are you doing!'—'Do you know where this was made?'—'Where else, America.'—'Honey, take a look at the manufacture?'—'Is this a joke?'—'I'm afraid not.'—'How did you find out?'—'A man was holding a sign that said $4.3 million were spent in 2007 importing American flags from China'—'You mean our government gave my godson, who fought and lost his life in Afghanistan, a false token of appreciation!'—'Yes.'"

"What did he do?"

"He threw it into the fire pit on the patio and burnt it."

They both listened to the rain as Myrtle recalled running the story a few months earlier. She wasn't surprised Virginia was just learning about it, but she felt it was better than never.

"Listen, Myrtle, I called because there's something I need to tell you."

She was somewhat excited because Virginia was always full of gossip.

"Sure."

Virginia exhaled deeply.

"We've been friends for some time, so I feel my concerns are legit."

"Is everything all right?"

"For a few months Gregory's been engaging in activities I feel are unsuitable. My balcony observes the entire street—including your house—so when I was reviewing material for a patient one night, a car had parked near your house. I brushed it off thinking it was for the neighbor, but when Gregory got in the car. I grew concerned."

Thunder shook both their houses.

Myrtle's skin crawled as the adrenaline knotted her stomach with nausea. Her mouth went dry, but she kept her voice from cracking. She felt warm and looked around because there was a sudden fear that someone was watching her.

"Are you sure about this?"

Virginia felt no regret.

"I didn't know what to think," continued Virginia. "When the occurrences happened more frequently. I figured it was one of Gregory's friends stealing their parents' Porsche for a joyride. So one night, I hid behind a tree to see if it was one of the kids from school."

"Was it?"

"No. It was someone much older than Gregory."

"Oh dear."

"I'm terribly sorry about this, but there's never a right time to unload things like this. You would do the same since I know how you feel about our children."

"Thank you. You made the right choice. I'll handle things from here."

"All right, Myrtle. Take care of yourself."

Myrtle sat frozen as the phone fell from her hand.

Flashes of lightning filled the sky as thunder silenced the house. She wished Virginia had never called, but how else would the situation been uncovered? Myrtle was called to act on parental duty, but somehow she wasn't ready for it.

The garage door opened, so she ran to the restroom and locked the door. She stared into the mirror and saw a fearless woman determined to overcome this hurdle.

Ten minutes passed and she was ready to face Josh.

When she entered the kitchen, he didn't suspect anything because Myrtle was exceptional at hiding her emotions. She kissed his cheek and asked him to join her in the living room. They were talking about their day when Gregory came down to get a drink of water. It took every ounce of energy to keep her passions from escaping her, but she needed to do this right in order to find out who this person was.

Later that night, she sat in the stillness as she pretended to sleep. Rage flowed through her as the walls creaked in the night.

Could it be drugs, prostitution, or something worse? she thought as she listened to her husband's breathing. It rid her body with anxiety as she closed her eyes. *This has to stop because Gregory has no reason to be involved in whatever he is doing.*

Soon her heart stopped and the edges of the door lit up before going dark again. She crept out of bed and stood at the window. The white Porsche pierced her with sadness.

It was one in the morning as Myrtle heard him moving downstairs. She placed every step with caution until the door was slowly opened. His cologne danced over her nostrils like ice, and she wanted nothing more than for Gregory to come back.

When the lock fastened, she bolted to the garage.

The vibrations from the road eased her as she discreetly followed them. They arrived to a tower of lofts, and the destination frightened her that much more. Once the delinquent car passed the security gate into the parking lot, she saved the plate numbers on her phone.

XII

PHOENIX

Friday, November 21, 2008: 1.00 a.m.

Dim lights reflected over stainless-steel appliances in the kitchen. Gregory hung his cashmere coat on the rack and leaped onto the black granite countertop. His sunflower-colored sweater absorbed his green eyes. His pink tongue moistened his lips before he spoke.

Organic whole milk was placed on the counter so it could be mixed with the cocoa powder in the machine.

Chocolate milk with whipped cream soon filled blue ceramic mugs.

"In Mr. Hickson's class today—my debate was the loudest yet."

"Really. I'd like to hear about that," I said.

A smirk lit the corners of his mouth.

"The class chose the topics from a hat. Mine was war."

"In general, or the Iraq War?"

"In general—so naturally I had an edge with that one."

"Sounds intense."

"John and I were called to the front of the class and Mr. Hickson said sternly, 'You guys have twenty minutes to defend your arguments. Gregory, are you for or against the topic?'— 'Against'—'Very well. George, prepare your defense while Gregory speaks.' Mr. Hickson placed his eyeglasses on his desk and looked at the clock. 'You may begin.'

"I turned to the class and felt alive because I lived for moments like these.

"'War is divided into three divisions: the front liners, the back liners, and the creators.

Innocence doesn't exist during these times—only death. War can change anyone into a machine of hate. It makes every man equal because fear rests upon their throats. Soldiers are trained to defend themselves and their country at any cost. Grievance is never allowed—just kill, or be killed. So when our soldiers come home—can we really expect them to be rational when all they've seen is death? War has no heart, so fantasy and reality do not exist during its reign. In the end—war will doom our race.'

"Mr. Hickson documented the time and looked at George.

"'Begin.'

"'War is a force that gives us meaning. Without it, empires crumble and we would fall into communist hands. Who wants equality with people not worthy of our ideologies? It's obvious our opponents think the same. So why fear it? Every day we rise we're faced with the reality that our lives could end anytime. We take medications to prolong existence—pray because we fear the unknown—eat healthy because we fear disease. War is no different…we fight to exist. If it wasn't for war, America would've never been born. It lets a country show its strength. Gregory may have said, 'War escapes no one,' but there's truth in that. Because if foreign invaders attacked us, activists wouldn't stop to think whether 'killing is wrong.' They would slice 'n' dice the enemy to preserve their existence. I'm not condoning murder, but in the right circumstances—war heightens our species.'

"The time was documented and we were asked to be seated."

"How does this kid have such a nightmarish vision?" I asked.

"He's one of the richest students at our school. The administration allows his weirdness to pervade because his family donates generously—and that's aside from tuition. He's a druggie who'll fry his brains before graduation, so no one really cares. But everyone was shocked to hear how composed his thoughts were."

Gregory lay on the sofa, so I lay next to him. I listened to his breathing as I ran my fingers ran through his hair.

"I got a bizarre letter from my brother the other day," said Gregory.

"Is he okay?"

"Yeah, but he's heartbroken because a friend of his died recently."

"What happened?"

"He said his friend was an international model from Italy, and last week she left to New York for a shot that was going to premiere her on the cover of *Vogue*."

"How cool that would've been."

"I know. I think it's freaky how she had fallen from her balcony the night before heading back to school."

"That is strange. Was it a suicide?"

"No. She was heavily intoxicated with traces of Rohypnol."

"Interesting."

"Nathan thinks someone at the bar drugged her, but the elevator camera didn't show her with anyone and the autopsy never found foreign bodily fluids."

"My friend from Cambridge has said when he visits New York he's always vigilant about his surroundings because various people were getting drugged with GHB."

"That's awful."

"A few men filed reports, but mainly it was woman who did. No one knew whether it was the bartenders or *seemingly* close friends with ulterior motives."

"My brother says a lot of people are confused because she was extremely anti-drug. The police said people with that level of Rohypnol are either raped or found dead to make it look like an overdose."

"How old was she?"

"Twenty."

"What a shame."

"It's incidents like this that give the field a bad rap. Because now that she's dead, the magazine isn't going to feature her on the cover."

"The publishing world is just as ruthless. A writer could spend their whole life writing only to have the world ask what's next before the work is even released."

"It can be hard to get ahead these days."

"Ah. But what does it mean to truly *get ahead?*"

"Well…you seem to be in that category."

"I disagree. I may be better off than most. But I am not immune to failure."

"If I could be a millionaire, I would still want to be in your shoes because—"

"Gregory. Money isn't everything because sometimes you have to work with unpleasant people."

"I would expect that comes with the territory."

The question made me think of Josh and how blunt he could be. It wouldn't be fair to insult Georgy's father, so I channeled the negativity to something positive.

"Not necessarily. Sometimes people forfeit the ladder-climb because the higher you go, people intentionally speak their mind to weed out the competition," I said.

"Do you come across that a lot?"

"I did in college, but not so much in my career. In the legal world people have strong opinions, but that isn't going to make you quit your job. If it does, you're in the wrong field. You got to be thick-skinned."

I believed people were entitled to their opinions no matter how offensive they were, just as long as they were based on facts, and not emotion.

"That makes sense, but I guess I'm more curious on how much bullshit you're willing to take before quitting. The point where even money loses your interest."

"We all have to put up with that no matter the field you're in. Some just have the luxury of stepping away from it when they want."

"Is that something you're able to do?"

"I couldn't when I was finishing my internships. But now I can, yes."

"Don't you think it would be interesting to see yourself if you had the chance to go back to those days? Or better yet, the chance to see how others see you?"

"That would be neat. But since I ran with the crowd, my perspectives weren't in the right place. It took a great deal of strength to reverse the self-destruction I was getting accustomed to."

"Things can get the better of us sometimes. It doesn't make us any less human," said Gregory.

"I agree. But you can't always see things eye to eye when you're lost."

"What sort of things were you doing?"

"The gay community has a way of convincing you that self-destruction is alluring."

"How unfortunate."

"That's just how it is sometimes."

Gregory moved toward me and pressed his lips on mine before he looked at the clock.

"Looks like it's that time again," he said.

"Is that so? What a shame."

He stood up and pulled me forward. The bedroom was illuminated by the skyline as he removed his clothing. He stood against the window as I licked my finger and slid it inside his ass. I put his cock in my mouth and tasted his precum as he moaned. I then picked him up and pressed his back against the glass while I penetrated him.

XIII

CONDEMNATION

Friday, November 21, 2008: 6.00 a.m.

Gregory arrived home as the sky turned gray. The dewy air was think with oak and mesquite. He immersed into the hallway as the grandfather clock chimed.

He held his breathe as he climbed the stairs. This never lost its difficulty whenever he snuck out.

He exhaled and pressed his back against the door. In the darkness, he approached the closet and placed the bag down.

He moved to the restroom and turned on the light. He met his mother's eyes in the reflection before she opened the closet to retrieve the bag.

Weakness spread to his knees. The items somehow gave her ease, because she didn't find anything suspicious.

She spoke softly so that her husband wouldn't be disturbed.

"What the hell is going on, Gregory?" shaking the bag with a clenched fist. "Why are you leaving in the middle of the night?"

He wasn't ready to reveal his lifestyle because getting caught would only taint it that much more.

How could he explain that the secrecy was to protect his family from the grief that was going to infect them?

Somewhere deep inside he hoped that love would prevail, but testing the merits of his family was still unknown.

Gregory broke with a rickety voice. "I was just out for a night stroll with some friends."

Her neck pulsed as her eyes became dry with irritation.

"At *six* in the morning! For Christ's sake, Gregory, if you keep lying, I'm going to wake your father—"

Gregory continued testing the water.

"I was with Jeanie."

"You've left me no choice—"

A desperate cry rang from his voice.

"I was with someone who's been nothing but understanding of me."

Her eyebrow arched.

"What's that supposed to mean?"

"I was with a man."

So Virginia was right, she thought as she looked away. Even though she already knew, she wanted to hear it from him.

Dawn slowly filled the room, but it only touched their agony.

"Do you have anything to say?" asked Gregory.

"No."

"You could at least look at me."

She turned and shot regret into his heart. The feeling of falling filled his gut.

"How could someone do this to themselves?" she asked.

"It's who I am."

"This *man* is twice your age."

Myrtle knew she leaked something that was supposed to stay secret, but all was lost when Gregory recognized the truth.

"Who told you that?"

"That's none of your business."

"The hell it isn't. How did you know that?"

She found herself at a crossroads that stretched beyond possibility as she ignored the question. *He's only a child—a child who's lost, a child I can't save. Where did I go wrong?* thought Myrtle as she stared at him.

"What exactly has this person done for you?"

"He doesn't *hold* me back."

"So your father and I do that?"

"You wouldn't understand."

She looked at her son as if she didn't know him.

"What is there to understand about a seventeen-year-old? Is he giving you money to sell your body?"

"No!"

"So this is consensual?"

"Yes."

Gregory always believed lies ruined people, but this time *truth* was going to condemn him. He felt if only his family had been open to alternative lifestyles things wouldn't need to be so secretive.

"How long have you been sneaking out?"

"Since April."

She turned her back and shook her head in disgust.

The silence between them was eerie. He could only stand and listen to its gravity.

"Gregory. There's no turning back once you've put away childish things, because a man who returns to it is a fool."

"This isn't a question about growing up. It's about truth."

"Very well, Gregory. If that's what you want—"

"It is what I want."

"Then if you agree to not see this man again. I won't tell your father."

"You expect me to do that?"

"Absolutely. If not. He'll decide what to do."

His heart could feel the phoenix rising in his bones.

"I can't believe you're saying this."

"It's simple enough, Gregory. The choice is yours."

She went downstairs and left the house. She moved across the yard to where no one could see her. The fog was thick as she cried against a tree. Trust would never come between them again and that saddened her. She looked forward to her children leaving home knowing what was best for them. But that was gone now.

She knew life didn't always produce answers, but this wasn't the outcome she bargained for when she decided to raise a family. This was one of the reasons she and Josh left Ithaca after college because the mindset back east was too fast to raise a family. She couldn't believe the type of perversion that seeped into her home after everything she believed in. She wasn't ready for the battle she thought she'd won years ago.

Gregory closed his bedroom door and collapsed into a pool of tears as he thought, *What have I done for them to turn their backs on me?*

XIV

NOVELTY

Thursday, November 27, 2008: 7.00 p.m.

A week later a bag was packed with clothes and items for a weekend. It was dinner time and soon Gregory would be called down.

"What will you do in Austin?" asked Myrtle.

"Jeanie and I want to walk around UT."

"But neither of you have interest in going there."

"I know. We plan to go rock climbing at the Greenbelt, swim at Barton Springs, and kayak around Town Lake."

"When will you leave?" asked Josh.

"After school tomorrow."

"Wasn't there a paper you were working on?" asked Myrtle.

"I finished last night."

"Why didn't you tell us sooner?"

"We didn't know till last night. Midterms aren't till next month, so we figured we could get away for a short weekend."

"Very well. How much money do you need?" asked Josh.

"Around three hundred."

"I'll leave the money and credit card on the credenza in the morning. If you're not back by sunset Sunday evening. I'll deduct the money from your allowance," replied Josh.

"Fair enough."

After dinner, everyone went to their rooms. Gregory put on "Far Too Frail" and opened his window. He sat on the ledge and called Jeanie.

"What you up to?" he asked.

"Just watching the news on mute. Had a brutal practice today."

"You ready for the NXN Nationals next month?"

"Oh yeah. Ever since the club qualified for the South Regionals. We're headed to the Finals."

"That's awesome. I bet everyone's excited."

"We lost the spot last year, so we we're pretty pumped about going to Portland this year."

"I should go support you guys."

"We're in the process of making reservations, so when I find out more, I'll let you know. Maybe you can fly with us so you can cheer from the course."

"Let me know, and I'll see what I can do."

"Are you done with homework?" she asked.

"Yeah. But there's something I wanted to tell you."

"Everything okay?"

"Yeah. I just need your help."

She sat up and lowered the stereo.

"What's going on?"

He looked at the door's gap to be sure the hallway light was off.

"I'm going to Austin tomorrow."

"What for?"

"Sightseeing."

"And you're going without me!"

The comment tightened his throat.

"Don't blow this out of proportion. I just have a lot on my mind and I need to clear my head."

"So do I, but you don't see me taking a vacation."

"Are you going to help or not?"

"For all the times I've covered for you, you think I would've gotten something in return already."

"Come on. Don't do this right now."

She sighed heavily.

"All right," she said heavily. "What am I going to do for you this time?"

"Come have breakfast at the house tomorrow so we can talk about the trip."

"Why?"

"My mother thinks you wouldn't lie to her, so if you're here. She won't question anything."

"Are you playing hooky?"

"No, I'm leaving after last period."

"All right. See you in a few hours."

The next morning the air smelt fresh and the sun seemed to have a sensation it never had. Jeanie sat at the table and her eye makeup was heavy. It looked seductive against her loafers and argyle socks. Their uniforms were meant to downplay fashion, but they found ways to distinguish themselves.

Mrs. Collins was known for her cooking, so the misfits laughed as they talked about the scandal while the smell of bacon seeped from the kitchen. When Myrtle came in, they helped her with the plates.

Mrs. Collins chewed on a piece of sausage before taking a sip of Pellegrino.

"What universities have you applied to, Jeanie?"

"A few Ivys. But my heart is set on Princeton. I'm sure Gregory's told you I want to study economics."

"Yes. I find that very interesting. I told your mother some time ago that we needed more woman economists in today's market. Your parents are very proud."

"Thanks, Mrs. Collins."

"How is Mrs. Gerhart lately?"

"Very busy. But she mentioned last night that she was going to call in a few days so the two of you can grab dinner."

"How lovely. Be sure to remind her we can go whenever she wants."

"I will."

After breakfast, he took the envelope from the credenza and kissed his mother good-bye. It was amazing how little their tensions could be seen after the incident. But Gregory knew the money was a type of bribery Myrtle tried to mask as loyalty. He felt it was best to make her think she'd won as he pretended to be cordial.

They walked outside and placed their arms over one another. Gregory placed his sunglasses on and sat in his car. "The Headmaster Ritual" blared from Jeanie's sapphire Mercedes 560SL as she lit a cigarette. The morning was fresh as they followed one another to class.

Once last period finished, Jeanie met Gregory by his black BMW E21. The wind tossed her hair over the aviator Ray-Bans as a stream of smoke slithered from her lips. They leaned against his car and watched the tennis team scrimmage in the courts.

"I still don't understand why you're going," she asked.

"Should it matter?"

"No. I just wish you would let me in sometimes."

Gregory kissed her cheek and set his book satchel in the trunk. His white oxford blazed in the sun as he untucked it.

"I'll call you when I get there."

"Yeah yeah. You owe me big," as she squashed the butt with her shoe.

The journey officially began when he turned onto the highway. Traffic wasn't thick, but once the skyline came into view, his heart swelled.

As planned, he called the person he met off Craigslist to meet at the Starbucks off 5th Street. Once there, he paid for the fake ID and proceeded to the hotel.

When he arrived, he parked the car by the entrance.

"Good afternoon, sir. Are you a guest or visitor?" asked the young valet in a light blue polo and tight pale yellow shorts.

"Guest."

The attendant took a pink slip from his back pocket.

"Here's the call number. Enjoy your stay."

Another attendant pulled at the glass door and the lobby smelt of fresh flowers and leather. He walked to the front desk and rested his bags by his feet.

"Welcome to the Four Seasons. Do you have a reservation?" asked the concierge with gentle hazel eyes. He was tall, young, and lanky with a professional edge. His tiny manicured mustache was blond and suited his personality.

"I don't, but I would like a room for two nights."

Gregory gave the clerk the necessary materials to check in, and soon he was in the elevator. When he arrived at room 904, he took his phone and stepped onto the balcony.

"Hello?"

"Hi, Mom. We've arrived in one piece."

"Oh good. Your father wanted to speak to you, but he's on a call right now."

"It's okay. We can talk tomorrow."

"How's Jeanie?"

"She's in the shower. Were about to order room service before we head out."

"You kids be careful."

"We will."

He sent Jeanie a text telling her he would call her tomorrow. He wasn't entirely sure how she was going to cover for him when his mother finally found out she wasn't here. But by the time that happened, Gregory hoped it would be weeks from now. He locked the door and decided to walk downtown. After dinner at a bistro, Gregory had some espresso at a coffeehouse and went back to the hotel.

There was no denying the immense freedom he felt as he stood on the balcony. He wasn't sure how the night would unfold, but he was excited to see another world. That sense of empowerment meant everything to him, and whenever someone preached that, they needed the experience to back their point.

The shower slowly filled with steam as he stared into the mirror. Gregory always enjoyed his physique, and swim practice did it justice. He knew the power his looks had as he masturbated to his reflection. When we came into his palm, he placed the semen in his mouth and ran his tongue along the mirror.

Once showered, he moisturized his skin and sprayed cologne over himself. He slipped on his loafers, pink shorts, and white V-neck shirt. It was eleven when he stepped into the elevator and stared at his reflection. Once he stepped into the night, he headed to the Warehouse District.

It would be his first time at a gay bar as he moved along the busy street filled with pedi-cabs. The deed was naïve, but there was bravery being alone. As he approached the large wooden doors, the music was already pumping against this body.

A tall, skinny fellow in a red wig with long green eyelashes greeted him. The glitter around his eyes made his yellow lips seem perky.

"Hey there, darling. You here all alone?"

"I am."

"That won't last long. Five dollars, please."

He reached into his wallet and fished for the ID.

"Don't you need to check this?"

"You're way above that, my dear. In time you'll understand why."

The drag queen placed the band around Gregory's wrist and laughed as he closed the register.

He moved into the club not knowing that men his age who weren't regulars stood out. The lure was easily addicting.

He felt eyes upon him in the smoky room. People paused their conversations to watch him pass. The absence of women was welcoming, and the atmosphere felt uplifting.

He moved to the bar and said, "I'll take a bottled water."

"One dollar," replied the shirtless bartender with spiky brown hair.

Violet, yellow, and red neon lights lit the room as shadows moved about the ceiling. Gregory moved to the outdoor patio to get some air. Five minutes later someone sat next to him.

"Hello there," said the stranger.

"Hi."

"Can I get you something to drink?"

He held up his wrist and said, "Sorry."

"They don't pay attention to that sort of thing here. Do you like whiskey or vodka?"

"Whiskey."

"Good," said the man as he held out his hand. "My name is Edgar."

"Nice to meet you. I'm Gregory."

When the man came back, he took the drink and savored it. Gregory didn't care much for cigarettes, so when the thirty-three-year-old started smoking, he left.

He went to the other side of the bar, and a twenty-eight-year-old man approached him. This time the conversation was a bit livelier, which led to a second drink. Once it was finished, Gregory needed to use the restroom. He was followed by two men who stood beside him to watch him urinate. They grew erect and stroked their cocks in hopes of seducing him.

Gregory found this highly uncomfortable, but erotic all the same. He moved into the club filled with neon beer signs clinging to the walls.

Gregory was going to grab another water when a hand patted his back. A tall, light, brown-eyed and -haired man smiled innocently. He was thirty and his intent to speak with Gregory was obvious.

"Hi. I'm Greg. Haven't seen you before. Where you from?"

"Around."

He laughed and recognized the defensive innocence. He then shot a gaze at the DJ booth.

"If you aren't here with anyone. I wouldn't mind buying you a drink. But first we need to do something."

"Like?"

"You'll see."

Intrigued. He followed him inside.

"Where did such a fine man come from?" asked the DJ.

"Different places."

"Me to," said the DJ as he touched Gregory's face before running his hand along his chest and stomach. "I'm Aiden."

Gregory blushed and looked at the dancing crowd.

"I'm Gregory."

"With a face like that—you don't need a name," as Aiden looked at Greg, who was behind Gregory. He nodded and a 21+ band was pulled from the drawer and replaced the old one.

"Now you can play with the big boys. Care for a shot?" asked Greg.

"Sure."

Vodka was pulled from under the desk.

Gregory left the booth and began to feel the alcohol take hold. Eager to try his new gift, he ordered a shot of whiskey and migrated into the crowd before Greg came beside him.

"You ever smoke Hydro?" he asked.

"No."

"Here. Let's go to the patio."

They shared the joint as people walked by and smiled. It was his first time smoking marijuana, so the effects were unfamiliar. After a few puffs, Greg put out the joint and placed it in a mini Altoids box.

They went back inside, where the base ran through their bones. It was intoxicating as everything began to blur. All that mattered was the music as it elevated his pulse. Go-go dancers wearing nothing but underwear jumped onto their blocks. It was one in the morning.

Gregory turned to tell Greg something, but he was gone. He continued dancing as his inhibitions faded. One of the dancers spotted him across the room and approached. He had crystal blue eyes, fair skin, supple red lips, and shiny blond hair. Gregory recognized the despondency, but his beauty countered the reality. Without words they locked lips beneath the flashing lights. "A Daisy Chain 4 Satan" started playing and Gregory couldn't believe it. Out of all places, he didn't think he would hear it here, but the beats meshed with the scene.

The dancer peeled Gregory's shirt off and tucked it behind his back. Not long after, Greg came up and sandwiched the couple so they could glide without reservation. People around them watched as the three began making out while massaging each other's erections.

Eventually, the dancer pulled away and took Gregory's hand. Greg followed as they moved into a restroom stall. A white baggie came into Gregory's distorted vision.

"What is that?"

"What do you think?" said the dancer. "A little blow to get the night started."

"Ever done this before?" asked Greg with yellow-green eyes.

"No."

The platinum blond grabbed Gregory's face and aggressively put his tongue in his mouth. He could feel his pants being unbuttoned as Greg took his cock into his mouth. The dancer pulled away and prepared a key for use. Gregory watched Greg until it was time to inhale the substance. After an assortment of bumps were inhaled, they did more shots at the bar. Last call was announced, but afterhours went on till 4 a.m.

Around two-thirty the dancers were released from the dance floor.

"Wanna come to our place?" asked the dancer.

"What's your name, by the way?" said Gregory.

"Does it even matter?" he said, laughing.

The small crowd standing outside the club looked at their shirtless bodies. Someone from the crowd asked if they could join, but Greg told them to fuck off.

"If it matters. I'm Owen."

"I'm Gregory."

"We driving or what?" replied Greg as he licked Owen's ear.

"No. My place is a few blocks down," replied Owen.

It was unusually humid as the three stumbled into the streets. Soon they were inside a high-glossed kitchen with black appliances. Shots were poured before the group moved to the living room. In a heavy sweat, they laughed as lines on the glass table were snorted. They stepped onto the balcony, feeling the night fresh upon their skin. Gregory was against the railing when a pair of hands touched his body.

When he turned around Aiden said, "Welcome home."

Gregory laughed and said he needed to use the restroom. He could hear them doing more blow as they giggled. He stared into the mirror when Kaskade suddenly pulsed through the condo. His image swayed as he couldn't recognize the person in the reflection. His heart raced as his tongue and eyes felt dry.

When he came out, Aiden took him into his arms and kissed his forehead.

"I think I've had enough for tonight," said Gregory.

Aiden had short black hair with smooth skin. His black eyes looked impatient and balmy. He leaned forward and whispered, "But I don't think you have."

"I don't do this sort of thing. I'm not even sure why I'm here."

Aiden looked at Owen and Greg before saying, "Neither do we."

Aiden persuaded him to stay as he unbuttoned Gregory's shorts. Greg switched off the lights and turned on a lamp with a red bulb. The ceiling spun as the three men surrounded him. Gregory lay on the floor as the spell took over him. They flipped Gregory on his stomach as the group took turns licking his anus. Owen applied lubrication onto his erection and eventually penetrated him.

Aiden turned Gregory's face so he could watch in the mirror. Owen thrust until he left his seed inside him. Greg quickly took over until Aiden pushed him away. Unaccustomed to girth, Gregory drooled with ecstasy as Aiden held his shoulders.

Greg slid his penis into Gregory's mouth as Owen watched and smoked a cigarette on a leather chair. Moments later Aiden climaxed and moved aside so Greg could also dispense his cum.

After the episode Aiden said, "While that was fun and all. It's time for bed and for everyone to leave."

Gregory staggered to put on his clothes. The orgy, drugs, and liquor had taxed him.

Just as the three were walking out, Aiden asked, "By the way. Since the cream puff doesn't know how to ask. He should know the three of us are negative. Does the same apply to you?"

Baffled by the question, Gregory answered with certainty, "Yes."

The door was shut before they moved along the sidewalk. They kissed Gregory good night and told him his hotel was two blocks south.

When he got to the room, he fell to his knees and began sobbing. He didn't know where to turn, so he called the one person he trusted.

"Hello?"

"Christian. Where are you?"

"Gregory. What's the matter?"

"What have I done? I'm sorry. I didn't mean to."

"What—where are you?"

"Austin."

"Austin! With who?"

"Myself."

"Where?"

"The Four Seasons."

"Are you hurt?"

"Yes. I need you! Where are you?"

"Don't move. I'm on my way."

"Hurry."

XV

CONCILIATE

Saturday, November 29, 2008: 5.00 a.m.

The drive along the interstate was bare. Nothing could drown the emptiness in my stomach. It was unlike Gregory to lose control.

There was something heavy in the air as the yellow lanes blurred. I didn't care how fast I was going because his safety was all that mattered. Soon the skyline burned against the turning twilight as I took the phone.

I stood in the empty lobby waiting for the elevator. His room was at the end of the red carpeted hall with silver trimming. When the door opened, he fell into my arms.

He was balmy and pale. Even his lips were colorless as his hair stuck to his face. Every breath was long and pronounced.

I laid him on the sofa and fetched some water. The room's view was proud as it gleamed in the background. I kissed him and brought the glass to his lips.

He burst into tears as he leaned into my chest. The convulsions in his throat made it difficult for me to remain composed even though I could feel his pain.

"Hey there, guy. You mind telling me what's going on?" I whispered into his ear.

"Oh, Christian. I can't believe it. I've ruined everything."

"You could never do that even if you tried."

"But I have."

"Can I ask what happened?"

"I had unprotected sex with three strangers."

Hearing that left no impression because I'd been guilty of that in the past. Answers could never be found once loneliness was at your side, so it was easy to empathize with him.

"I wish you hadn't done that. But it doesn't change how I feel about you."

"I thought the situation could be contained. But everything happened so fast."

"Why did they make you come here?"

"They didn't. I just met them tonight."

I softly smiled and ran my thumb over his eyebrow.

"Where did you go?"

"Boyz Cellar."

"Did you go alone?"

"Yeah," as he swallowed coarsely. "There's something I'm not telling you."

"I would like to know if you don't mind."

"You remember how you told me after your divorce you went on a party binge?"

"Yes."

"Well, I wanted to do the same."

"Why? You know I don't speak highly about the scene."

"Well there's more," placing his hand at my arm. "Christian. My mother found out about us."

There was a part of me that hoped we would never be discovered. But from the beginning we knew the truth could turn dry.

"Did she say how?"

"No. But when I came home last weekend she was waiting in my room."

"I see."

"I told her about the relationship, but since she knows everything about you, she wouldn't hear anything about it."

"She works in publishing. I'm sure she has plenty of resources."

"Possibly. But the good news is that she hasn't told my father."

"That's odd."

"She said if I stopped seeing you she would bury the secret."

"Is that going to happen?"

"No. We can figure something out. But sneaking out isn't going to work anymore if we're going to continue visiting one other."

"Did she say anything else?"

"No. But then again she didn't mention anything about you being business partners with my father."

"We have to keep it that way. Your father works with a lot of people, so I'm sure my name didn't sound familiar."

"I know. But there has to be a way for us to communicate."

"Agreed," as I leaned to kiss him. "Now I see why you're here."

"I'm so angry at her that I went out to get in trouble."

"Well now that that's out of your system. Let's try to keep it together."

"I can't stand how she pretends she isn't hurting me. Every day I feel this underlying tension when she looks at me. I don't want to be there anymore."

"Just a few more months and you'll be free. If your mom wants to live in denial—then let's play along. But tonight isn't how I want you dealing with problems."

"I'm really sorry."

"I understand that. But what you got sucked into is a serious problem for a lot of people. Booze, sex, and drugs glamorizes self-destruction. It's the perfect concoction for people with self-esteem issues to pass the time, but the issues will always remain. You know how drug use disgusts me."

"I know. Everything just sort of happened."

"What I want you to realize is that once you get over this hurdle, you won't need to numb the void with things that cause more pain. Even if your parents don't meet you halfway, at least you can say you tried. Families don't always get along, so just because something doesn't go your way doesn't mean you should fall apart. If that's the case, you have to ask who's the one being close-minded if you're forcing things upon them."

"I see."

"Does that make sense?"

"Yeah."

"Now that you got a taste of the scene. Do you see I wasn't exaggerating?"

"I think its wild how vanity has a mind of its own."

"Many don't escape it because promiscuity is so natural to men," I said.

"Why do you think gay men are so aggressive about it?"

"They try to account for the masculinity society deprives them."

"I can see that."

Reluctance swayed in his eyes, so I had to be sure he understood what was being conveyed.

"Do you remember that couple Jeanie told you about?" I said.

"Yeah."

"Do you understand why they fell into that trap?"

"Sort of."

"Most relationships bring that clubbing element onboard because they can't imagine living without it. It helps them feel young when they experience it."

"I found it concerning how they had everything, yet this eternal thirst to pursue sexual conquests dominated their lives," he said.

"Not all couples are prone to open relationships. If one wants it and the other doesn't, the one who does—lies about it—all the while they're pursuing flings behind their partner's back."

"It seems like no one is capable of being happy."

"For many, the adrenaline is so addicting that the chase is worth more than fidelity. People treat it like a scoreboard because after the bait is caught, they'll never see the same catch for another episode."

"How come?"

"The excitement's only present in the first encounter. After that—you're just a number no matter how much they want to get together again."

"Are you referring to young guys, or older men too?"

"Both. There are plenty of sixty-year-old men still chasing twenty-year-olds like nymphets."

"That sounds childish."

"It's the reason that patient had a breakdown. A lot of guys are so frustrated meeting people who don't want to be domesticated, that when they do. They quickly get attached."

"With certain parameters, I'm sure."

"Of course. Gay men are so hung up on looks and money they would pass on a young, smart guy with a great body and little money. For someone who was loaded even if they weren't smart or fit," I said.

"So what are young guys seen as?"

"A piece of meat unless they're really successful."

"I sort of got that vibe tonight."

"It's why drugs are so prevalent in the community. You'll always be seen like an object unless you run a commercial business or are some kind of celebrity. It wears on you when you can't measure up to anything for those reasons. It's pretty traumatic."

"I can imagine."

"I don't look down on anyone who practices open relationships, but it's what everyone does these days. Promiscuity isn't irrational anymore. It's a form of self-expression."

"Do you think we'll do that?"

"I hope not. Our relationship is too new to be discussing that. But then again the future isn't known until it happens."

"Whatever it ends up holding. It doesn't change that I feel bad about tonight."

"You weren't in the right state of mind. You've had a lot of pressure to deal with lately. So it's excusable."

"Thank you, Christian."

I could have told Gregory anything to make him feel better. But I told him the truth since he functioned heavily on it. Other people would've lied to him just so they could continue using him for sex, but we weren't about that.

I didn't want him becoming jaded like so many gay men do after the scene wrung them out. It was imperative he felt comfortable no matter what he pursued. We needed to lessen the blow his parents created because his wounds needed mending.

It was relaxing to see that his tension subsided even though shock was still in his eyes.

"Did they mention anything about their status?" I asked.

"They said they were negative."

A sigh of relief washed over me.

"Good. And for what it's worth. Did you at least enjoy yourself?"

"I did."

"Fair enough," I said while taking his hand. "Since I'm here. What would you like to do tomorrow?"

"Maybe we can have brunch. Then go kayaking afterwards."

"Sounds like a plan."

We were tired, so we moved to recharge in each other's arms.

But as Gregory slept, I recalled a conversation I had with John the other evening. For some reason we discussed the same topic, but it was about Mathieu. Since he passed away at the beginning of their relationship, John wondered how things would've unfolded.

We knew open relationships were becoming more common as social media devoured the bar scene. But we didn't want that life for us. So John was happy that Gregory and I were together because he knew the importance of companionship despite his recent loss.

XVI

FORESHADOWING

Thursday, December 18, 2008: 12.00 p.m.

The role of parenthood was testing its boundaries. No matter the issue—she was to love her son. She couldn't understand the motivation behind his choice because it frightened her.

Her disappointment streamed from her eyes as she thought of Gregory. Her mind drifted nowhere while her body ached. She felt helpless.

What brought this on? She and Josh had given him everything: money, clothes, furniture, a car. Why this?

What was he receiving that he couldn't get from home? Why didn't he feel complete?

But the more she pondered, she realized Christian was the problem. Not the family. What would motivate a thirty-year-old man to get involved with a seventeen-year-old? She believed Christian wanted to trick Gregory into believing deceit as truth. In her eyes Christian was someone who didn't get what he wanted out of life, so his need to corrupt youth was the only thing that could satisfy him.

The Collinses' nature was to protect themselves from the rotting world. But that somehow became the glitch in Myrtle's eyes and that devoured her.

♌

Josh reviewed files with a rose-hip candle burning at his desk. A fresh cup of organic silver-needle tea steamed beside him.

The office phone rang.

"Yes—"

"Derek, line two."

"Thank you," as he silky gripped the receiver with a smile. "Not home one day and you're already bugging me."

A boisterous laugh filled the earpiece.

"We're at the St. Regis. We decided to stay for a night before heading back. It wasn't planned, but when we arrived at JFK, we skipped the connecting flight.

"How was the trip?"

"Paris was great. The energy there has a warmth I never feel in the States."

"I agree. What's the mindset there right now?"

"It was interesting to say the least."

"How come?"

"Many of the Parisians are feeling the strain on tourism ever since ticket prices inflated on international travel. It's pinched everyone's wallets."

"I wouldn't doubt it. France's rising budget deficit has clamped everyone's spending."

"Not only that, but Germany is under pressure to enact a stimulus package and Britain is also struggling with a slumped housing market."

"The mood in Europe is just as gloomy as it is here."

"Very grim circumstances for a lot of people right now."

"I know. The global economy isn't looking good right now."

Derek wrinkled his nose as if he smelt something foul. He looked at his watch and said, "Listen, I would love to talk but I told my wife I wouldn't be longer then fifteen minutes."

"Where did you leave her?"

"Downstairs at the bar."

Josh chuckled and remembered how Derek was notorious for making people wait.

"All right. See you when you get back."

Josh turned to the skyline and stood in front of the window. He remembered the first time he and Myrtle went to the St. Regis after he won his first federal trial.

The intercom beeped again—stirring him from his thoughts.

"Yes—"

"Myrtle, line two."

He smirked and thought, *How could she possibly know I was thinking about her?*

He moved to his desk and grabbed the receiver.

"Hello?"

"How are you?" she asked.

"I'm following up on a trial coming up next week. Apparently a woman killed her neighbor's daughter because her hair was growing faster than her daughter's."

The response left her tongue dry and heavy as she paced the room.

"How unfortunate."

"She's pleading insanity. But I won't let her get away with that."

"I hope not."

"Don't worry, honey. Someone like that doesn't deserve the insanity card."

She crossed her legs and assembled the strength to not crumble into a million pieces.

"There's something I need to speak to you about," she said clearing her throat.

"You okay?"

Even though Myrtle had known about Christian for a few weeks. She had to pretend as if she had just learned about him. Even though they shared the same views about homosexuality, she still wanted to protect his pride.

"Virginia called last night with some news."

"Is she okay?"

"Our son has been sneaking out lately."

"Honey, Nathan's visiting from college. He's entitled to act like an adult. Have you already forgotten about your wild days?"

A dizzying momentum moved the room as her lip quivered.

"I'm referring to Gregory."

Josh frowned with a light irritation.

"Why is Virginia spying on us? Doesn't she have kids to raise?"

Myrtle would've felt the same way, but after pondering the situation, the news relieved her because there was no telling what would've happened without the intervention.

"I'm sure he's just scratching an itch since Christmas break is coming up," Josh said. "We'll have to talk to him about this because he knows we wouldn't approve of this."

"Josh. There's more."

His forehead wrinkled with deep crevasses. He knew something wasn't right because she sounded distant.

"Is he talking to a girl we haven't met yet? You know how boys get when they start dating."

Even though Gregory stopped sneaking out, he started arriving late, pretending he was studying with Jeanie at the library. She eventually called Mrs. Gerhart to see if Jeanie was with him, but it was obvious she wouldn't lie to Myrtle. She had warned him about the repercussions if he continued to disobey, but since his heart felt otherwise—so did hers.

"Not exactly—last night I stayed up to follow the car Gregory was in."

"Does he know you did that?"

"No," clearing her throat. "Since I'm good friends with the constable, I told him I received a lead from someone I wanted to know was legit, so I had him run the plates."

He wanted Myrtle to stop speaking because he knew his children knew better than to start trouble. Josh took a deep breath and proceeded with concern.

"Well—who was it?"

"A man who's been having *relations* with Gregory."

The word relations stung like poison.

"How do you know this?"

"After he came home, I snuck into his room and read his texts."

They knew the invasion of privacy was violating. But the circumstances called for desperate measures.

"What name came up from the plates?"

"Christian Wall."

Reality fell heavily on his chest.

"Wall. Christian Wall. You have to be mistaken."

"But I'm not."

"It must be a coincidence then. Derek and I trade business with him periodically," he said, rubbing his temples. "What car were they in?"

"A white Porsche."

Feeling sick, he stood up and loosened his Riccardo Tisci tie.

"Has Gregory lost his mind? I didn't raise him to be a mustache lover."

The fluid in her ears made her nauseous.

"What should we do?" she said confidently.

Josh flared like burning coal.

"I'm going to castrate Christian's balls—and eat them in front of him. This scumbag is the type of person who retards humanity."

Hollow breaths breathed from both ends of the line.

"Josh, I'm not trying to diminish the importance of the matter. But we can't divide our family for other people's mistakes. I don't want our family to be known for something like this."

"What are you suggesting then? Tell Christian to politely go away!"

"Let's speak with Gregory first. I'm sure he'll have an answer."

"As far as I'm concerned, he's had his chance to talk. But didn't."

Myrtle rested her head into her hand.

"Why don't you come home?"

"Not now. There's something I need to take care of first."

"Josh. You have people who love you. Don't do anything stupid."

"I'll be home later this evening."

Myrtle moved to the window and recalled how she and Josh had gossiped about people at the spa over the years. They felt it was harmless even though they were being critical. But now that the tables were turning, she wasn't entirely sure how to process the turn of events.

♌

The elevator door parted and I emerged into a large room with leather furniture and marble tile. Sabrina, my secretary, had long straight brunette hair that swayed with every step. Her red and green dress hugged her zero waist as she walked beside me.

"I tried convincing my mother to marry him, but ever since she went through the divorce with my father, she's skeptical about the whole thing.

But I don't want her being alone anymore," she said.

"Give her time."

"After we had dinner with him a few times—I think he's perfect for her. I mean, if the man wasn't twenty years older than me, he would be perfect for me."

We filled the lobby with laughter as I waved at the secondary secretary typing at the desk. Her blue eyeshadow and fire-orange hair gave her red lips appeal.

"Who's to say he isn't," I said.

"Please, I'm too young for a committed relationship. When I find my man, you'll be first to know."

"All right, Sabrina, it was good having lunch again."

"No problem."

I went into my office and closed the door. I put my jacket over the chair and opened a file. An hour had passed when there was commotion in the lobby. The yelling grew louder until the doors flung open.

Josh rushed toward me and I became paralyzed. He grabbed my shirt and pinned me against the window.

His breath moistened my face as the veins in his neck protruded like slugs beneath his skin.

"Did you honestly think I wouldn't find out?"

I wanted to push him off me, grind his face into the ground, but I knew better then to push a man while he was angry.

"Calm down and tell me what's going on. I can't help you if I don't know what's going on."

The secretaries entered the office.

"Should I call Security?" asked Sabrina.

I peeked over his shoulder.

"That won't be necessary. You can close the door."

Once the door clicked, he flung me to the floor and dug his knee into my chest.

"I guess you need a little refreshing then. Does Gregory ring a bell?"

The room spun as if I were heavily inebriated.

"It does."

"Good. Because I'm going to obliterate you in court. So enjoy your freedom while you can."

"Do whatever you need to."

"You pieces of shit are all the same. Why can't *any* of you ever learn?"

He spit in my face and walked to the entrance.

The secretaries came in with a panic and ushered me to my feet.

"Don't worry. Josh and I just had a little disagreement, that's all."

They led me to my desk and handed me a glass of water.

"Are you sure? I've never seen him like that."

"It's just a misunderstanding, girls."

"You should press aggravated assault charges."

"Ladies. There's no need to jump to conclusions," as I quenched my thirst. "So if you don't mind. I would like to be alone right now."

Their gazes loomed with perplexity.

"If you need anything, we'll be here for the rest of the afternoon," added the other secretary.

The silence was violating as I realized the gravity of the situation. Was he bluffing, or was he really going to challenge me?

I moved to the sink and rinsed my face. It was one o'clock and Gregory would soon be breaking for lunch. Nerves pounded my skull because I hadn't the vaguest idea what to do.

John eventually came to mind because another outlet was needed. I wasn't sure how to ask if he could visit for another weekend. But if he couldn't, his doctoral studies would be reason enough.

Either way, this was life and sometimes adversary was faced alone.

XVII

RUMBLE

Thursday, December 18, 2008: 8.45 a.m.

"I pledge allegiance to the Flag of the United States of America, and to the Republic for which it stands, one Nation, under God, indivisible with liberty and justice for all."—"Now our Lord's Prayer."—"In the name of the Father, the Son, and the Holy Spirit. Amen—Now for the morning's announcements—"

The student body sat down as the intercom continued barking.

Mr. Hickson wrote on the blackboard: "Midterm Paper Topics."

"—have a wonderful day."

The intercom went flat and Mr. Hickson addressed the class.

"We are on a liturgy schedule, so we won't have our usual time. I'll be quick in explaining my expectations for the papers due after Christmas break." Everyone laughed in union. "Folks. The holiday doesn't start till after seventh period, and I believe we're still in third."

The class went silent.

He walked to the window and faced the trees along the west side of campus.

"Everyone should follow these directions down to the bone: no exceptions. The papers are due the day classes convene. For every day a paper is late, five points will be deducted from the final letter grade in May."

The class groaned and hooted as Mr. Hickson adjusted his glasses with an index finger. His hair and beard had been freshly cut.

"If we want to complain. I'll make that ten."

He handed out the papers, and binders and hole-punchers filled the room.

The topics weren't in order of importance: How did social media influence the elections between Obama and Clinton? Should illegals be allowed to use health care? Was the election covered fairly by the media or was it biased? Should the government have bailed out Fannie Mae and Freddie Mac? Should sanctuary cities offer criminal illegals asylum or immunity from death penalties? Should drug-trafficking illegals have the right to press charges against US Border Patrol agents like Ramos and Compean, thus leading to eleven- and twelve-year prison sentences in 2006? Expand on why the Supreme Court's ruling on *Gonzales v. Carhart* started the erosion of *Roe v. Wade.*

Gregory looked out the window and saw two Marist brothers crossing the courtyard in their clergy black habits. It was amusing how it made them look as if they were floating on air.

The bell rang and everyone reached for their jackets and sweaters. It was cold out as the student body migrated toward the chapel.

Gregory walked beside Jeanie while fog emitted from their lips.

"Today couldn't have come any sooner."

"I know. It always gets crazy before vacation. It's been like this since seventh grade, yet we still spaz out."

"A half day with a liturgy schedule—the day couldn't have been any shorter."

Jeanie looked up as a gust of wind blew past them. She squealed with embarrassment as she held down her skirt.

"That's the only thing I hate about these fucking uniforms. The wind tries to find its way into every crevice."

Tilting his head back with laughter. He saw a frown upon his beloved companion.

"Why are you looking at me like that?" he asked.

"I don't find that funny."

"You knew a front was coming in. You should've worn pants."

"I wanted to wear my new stockings because we hardly get weather like this."

"You just wanted to show off those legs since your club won first place at the NXN Nationals."

"We didn't want it any other way."

"I'm just glad I got to see it all go down."

"Me too," as she adjusted her sweater. "I thought you were going to call last night."

"I was, but I fell asleep. Did you stay up late?"

"Yeah, I figured that much, so I ended up watching *The Doom Generation* again."

"Sweet."

The church bell tolled in the gloomy morning. One by one everyone took a place along the wooden bleachers and chairs. The purple altar sat against the burning candles under the shield-shaped stained glass window.

It was the third week of Advent and the air smelt of frankincense. A smell both Gregory and Jeanie enjoyed. When the musical precession began, everyone stood up. Once the priest ascended the altar, he motioned for everyone to sit down.

"Welcome. It's good to see you on such a fine day," said the priest.

Gregory leaned over and told Jeanie, "I wonder what the homily will be on today."

"I know, they're interesting enough that they could make a believer out of me."

"Now there's a bet I could win."

"Really?"

"Oh yeah."

"Don't hold your breath on that one."

♌

The gentle breeze rustled the leaves as Gregory and Jeanie sat down for lunch.

Sometime later his phone vibrated.

I pictured Gregory smiling as his hair rustled in the wind. Hearing him was going to be hard because today had already become a memory and he had the vaguest idea about that.

He excused himself and walked away.

"Hi."

"How are you?" I said.

"Just having a quick bite before class."

"Any plans for tonight?"

"Nathan and I are going to watch *The Reader* at the movies tonight. What about you?"

"I'll be running last-minute errands. You know, petty stuff to waste time."

"Procrastination, huh. Not good."

"Yes, I know."

"Are we still on for tomorrow?"

I took a deep breath and closed my eyes.

"Gregory, as much as I want to see you, it's not going to be possible anymore."

"What—how come?"

"Your father found out about us today."

"Are you serious? How?"

"I'm not sure, but he came to the office today."

"What did he say?"

I didn't want to tell him about the fight because it would've only made matters worse.

"He's going to press charges."

"Oh no."

"I'm terribly sorry about this, but I wanted to tell you before you got home."

I could hear the bell ringing in the background.

"I don't know what to say," he said softly.

"You and I said this could happen."

"I know. It's just—"

"Your parents may come from different beliefs, but they love you dearly. This is the outcome that stems from that. What matters is that we know the truth."

I knew the crossroads he was at because the transition into manhood was never easy.

"Whatever they have to say, I won't listen. We can run away together."

"Oh, Gregory. As much as we would like that, you need to finish school so you can go to college."

"This isn't fair. I hate them. In fact, I've always hated them."

"Now's not the time to get angry."

"I'll put a stop to this. I'll make my dad back down. You watch."

"Do what feels right since that's all there is of you."

"We'll get through this, Christian. I promise."

"You should get to class. The last thing we need is for you to get in trouble for truancy. But if they cut our communication—know it was worth it. Worth every damn minute."

"There's only a few months left. After that, they can't stop us."

"I know."

"I love you."

"I love you too."

The line went dead and despair consumed Gregory.

Where to now? he thought. *Life isn't supposed to be this way.*

He flinched when a hand touched his shoulder.

"Fuck! Why aren't you in class?"

Jeanie looked dislodged.

"For the same reason you're not. Who was that?"

"No one."

"Really? Then why are you sweating?"

"I have a lot going on right now."

"So that makes it okay to lie?"

"Jeanie. It's complicated."

Her eyes tried reading his expressions, but the distance was too far. She wished he had been closer, and that made her all the more concerned.

"So we'll get detention for being late. Big deal. Just tell me what's eating you."

Gregory picked up his bag and looked into her eyes with defeat. He knew she wasn't going to be happy about the secret being kept for so long, but there was nothing friendship couldn't overcome.

XVIII

Unraveling

Thursday, December 18, 2008: 6.00 p.m.

The day turned black under winter's wrath as Gregory moved into Jeanie's car. Sleet trickled from the sky.

He looked at her and saw a light he'd never seen before.

"I'm sorry for never explaining any of this to you," he said.

"I'm surprised. But then again this is you we're talking about."

"I'm difficult, I know."

"I don't find anything wrong with what you're doing. But that's because I know you. People frown on things like this. I'm surprised your parents haven't killed you yet."

"Some help you are."

"Gregory. You're going against something that will crush you."

"But I'm not trying to. Doesn't anyone get that?"

"Maybe some would've if you told the truth from the beginning."

"Well, if I don't feel like talking about something. I shouldn't have to."

"Fine. Then don't."

"Jeanie. I don't mean like that."

"Okay. Just no more secrets moving forward."

"Deal."

She kissed his cheek and hugged him.

"Don't worry, we'll get through this," she said.

Gregory climbed out and swung his backpack over his shoulder.

"I'll call you later."

She drove off and left Gregory in the sleet.

He started at the house. Its structure felt cold, distant, and unreal. Nothing could've prepared him for this.

He touched the knob and stepped into the foyer. Voices from the living room fell silent and desolation saturated the air.

"Gregory, is that you?" asked his father.

He moved to the living room, where his mother sat with crossed legs and his father stood behind a chair. The fireplace burned and stifled the room with oppression.

"I assume you already know what's going on?" Josh asked.

"Yes."

"Is there an explanation for it?"

"Yes."

"So you've put an end to it."

"No."

Josh looked at him like a nocturnal animal.

"Why not?"

"Why should I?"

"Because you know better."

Gregory felt like an island smoldering with fire.

"Do I now?"

The lump in her throat tightened against her rigidness. They had taught him to civilly defend himself if he was ever threatened.

"Honey, our interference is in your best interest—"

"You haven't known my interests for years!"

"*Their* world is full of regret, pain, and loneliness. They consume one another without reason. I won't stand for that," she added.

"So that gives you the right to know what's best for me?"

"Give me your phone then," Josh demanded.

"Why?"

"Because it's shit, and you don't pay the bills."

"No."

Myrtle walked over and held out her hand.

"Now!"

He did as he was told and folded his arms.

"We can't have you talking to anyone right now. At least until we knock some sense into you," she said as the phone was placed in her purse.

"The only sense you're capable of perceiving is selfishness."

Josh wiped the sweat from his brow. Contempt burned beneath skin as he wasted his energy on his family.

"Damn it, Gregory. We're being serious. If anyone thought you were carrying on like you had our approval—that could've jeopardized our jobs."

"I don't see anyone paying attention but you."

When Virginia followed up on the situation, Myrtle never told her who the stranger was. From the beginning, Myrtle wasn't happy that her parental skills were being judged. But she had to play the good neighbor and return her messages when she called. Myrtle had easily told Virginia that Gregory met some kids from another school, but she quickly put an end to the fraternizing so Virginia's curiosities could be appeased.

"Do you realize someone could've called CPS? There's no telling where this could've gone," she said.

"So you're lashing out because that's what everyone wants?"

"Quit trying to outsmart your way out of this. No one is above the law," Josh said excitedly.

"So if he was my age you wouldn't care?"

"Of course we would," said Josh.

"Why?"

"Because we don't agree with that behavior," Myrtle added.

"And I don't agree with how you're treating me."

Since they knew how people felt about homosexuals, Gregory and Christian thought it was amusing how they were meddling with pederasty.

He saw his mother's eyes avert behind Gregory. He turned and found Nathan behind him moving like a shadow to the other end of the room.

Their father turned with gritted teeth.

"We will tell you as we please, young man," filling his chest with air. "Shall we try this again?"

Gregory burst and shook them from their comfort.

"I don't care if you see me like a disease. But if that's how you want it—I'll act like one!"

Josh wanted to charge at him, but restrained himself because he wanted to set an example for Nathan.

Josh couldn't understand how someone could attack the entity that raised and supported them. The treachery was painful, but Josh was accustomed to punishing disobedience.

"If that's what you want to hear, fine. You're a disgrace to look at. A real son wouldn't let a man put his filthy hands on him to experience lust. You're too young to know about true love."

"And you think you do," he said with a laugh. "Well, let me tell you how the Internet has allowed me to speak with all sorts of people. I'm not entirely sure you would approve of our conversations, so I'll spare you the details."

"Do you even know the types of things gay men get into?"

"That's the whole point. I'm with Christian because I know how degenerate they can be and I don't want any part of it."

Myrtle stomped her foot on the floor.

"This man only wants one thing from you. You can't grasp that now, but after this clears— you'll see."

"Can't you see I don't care?"

No one in the family understood where Gregory was coming from because they were so opposed to the idea of same-sex relationships. Josh felt desecrated because the very people he despised ended up being his own flesh and blood.

Nathan stood up and said, "You're hypocrites. You expect us to respect those with different views—but you're not doing that. It doesn't make sense."

Myrtle ground her teeth and spoke through them. "Stay out of this."

"No. Both of you hate when others disagree with you. This isn't any different."

Josh hunched over as he dug his nails into the leather chair. His hair was damp and his eyes were red with irritation. He didn't feel remorse for anything he said because his achievements made him believe that he was fulfilling his destiny.

"I've hear enough from you, Nathan. Go to your room or keep quiet."

Gregory's face shined from his brother's support.

"Keep the smirk all you want, boy. When this is all over, don't crawl back when you need money. You're a lost cause trying to prove self-worth. But you'll never convince me that your conclusions have any merit."

Josh tried to manipulate Gregory. But he saw past it and it made him all the more enraged.

"I've never felt so free before, and you want me to give that up because people disagree with what I'm doing—to hell with that. I'd rather swallow than spit to that one."

"Really! I don't see you doing either of that right now," said Josh.

"That's how good I am that you missed it."

Josh pointed his finger with maniacal eyebrows. It was the first time the family saw the rage that fueled his ambition.

"What a repulsive thing you've become."

"You're just jealous because I won't let you in my world."

"Trust me. There's nothing to be jealous about."

"Good. Then I won't have to worry about forgiving you."

Everyone stared at Gregory as he stormed to his room. Nathan opened the closet and put on his jacket.

"Where do you think you're going?" asked Josh.

"If you don't mind. I'm going for a walk."

After the door closed, Josh moved to the kitchen and left Myrtle alone.

She felt the world's weight on her shoulders as she stared at the crackling fireplace. She couldn't believe the family had unraveled after everything they'd invested. She had done what everyone told her to do, and yet they were paying for wanting stability. It was upsetting how this time last year everything had been perfect.

XIX

DREAMING

Thursday, December 18, 2008: 10.00 p.m.

Gregory lay in bed. Tears glistened on his face with heaviness in his chest.

There was a knock at the door.

"Go away," Gregory implored.

The door opened and Nathan stepped in with the house cat.

Gregory turned to face the wall. He could smell his brother's cologne as Nathan reached for a blanket on the chair. He draped it over his shoulders and listened to the wind. The air was cold outside and it seemed to want inside the house.

Nathan spoke softly, hoping to ease his brother's concern.

"What happened out there isn't us. I didn't expect them to act like that."

Gregory raised his voice and rattled Nathan. "They're cowards."

"You were living a secret life. Who knows, maybe they would've taken it differently if you said something sooner."

"Didn't you hear what Dad said? Of course he wouldn't."

"He probably said that to scare you."

"That wasn't the first time he's made snarky remarks about gay people."

"What else has he said?"

"That the government had no right to interfere with AIDS in the '80s. He said it was doing its duty."

"I know. I've heard similar things. I'm sorry you had to hear that."

"At least I know where Mom and Dad stand. I don't care that I feel differently about them anymore."

Nathan loved his brother, but he wasn't entirely sure how to console him considering the circumstances.

"I don't believe that," he said.

"I shouldn't have to respect them just because they provide for me. If you ask me… that's bizarre."

"There's more to it than that."

Gregory turned around and saw his brother's concern.

"Like what?"

"For one, I didn't know about Christian until tonight. It didn't seem like you would've kept something like this from me."

"So what? It's my life."

"We've never had secrets in the family. This is why the situation looked worse than it did."

"That's no longer my problem."

"That doesn't diminish the fact they had reason to know about your intentions. I mean— why you?"

"If you're going to ask—don't. He and I agree pedophiles should fry on the electric chair."

"Gregory. That wasn't what I was thinking."

"Then what were you?" as he turned from the wall. "I'm going to be eighteen August 15th. This is just an excuse to punish me because I'm not abiding by their prescribed love. I wouldn't be surprised that if I agreed to never speak with Christian again, Dad wouldn't press charges. But since I'm defending him, Dad wants to fight me."

"Don't interpret this as betrayal," said Nathan.

"Of course it is. They took advantage of my trust."

"Can't you see they're not doing this because they hate you—"

"So they are because they love me?"

A gust of wind brushed the limbs as they scraped the roof. Gregory thought if he had taken his mother's offer, would this have happened? He felt selfish because he could've protected Christian by never getting involved, but this was beyond what he expected. Gregory felt the retribution came from their hatred for homosexuals, and they weren't going to spare anyone.

"Did you know he worked with Dad?"

"Yes."

"Didn't you find that weird?"

"No."

"Not even the age difference?"

"What example can be made from this? I'm not thirteen. This doesn't make sense."

"Illogical, as it may seem. They have to protect their investments regardless if they side with you. A lot could've gone wrong if someone found out."

"It already went to shit."

"Then tell me what you would've done if Mom and Dad lost everything?"

"So now you're lecturing me."

"I want you to understand they made you who you are. Without their recourses you would've gotten nowhere."

"So that gives them the right to abuse me."

"No."

"Why are they then?"

"If they are, what are you going to do about it? Run away while everyone picks up the pieces?"

"None of us wanted this, but this is what happens when opinions matter."

"You've definitely made that clear."

"I've done nothing to deserve this. And neither has he. The world is fucked up, and I hope everyone burns in it."

"I'm really worried about you and I wish I could stay until everything blows over, but I have to head back to school soon. There's no telling the kind of stress Mom and Dad will be under, and we know how that can be."

"If they keep to themselves. All the better."

"I would talk to them if I could. But you know they wouldn't listen."

"I know."

Nathan wanted to sit by him, but he was afraid to anger him further.

"If things get ugly, you can text or call whenever you want. Even if it's three in the morning. I don't want you doing this alone."

Gregory felt the generosity. It was going to be the first time the family would experience a crisis, and Gregory wanted Nathan to stay. But admitting that would worry him, and he didn't want to seem needy.

"You don't have to worry about me. I have someone to lean on while you're gone."

"I'm serious when I'm asking you to stay connected because I know how you clam up when things get rough."

Gregory turned and faced the wall again.

"I don't want to talk about this anymore."

Nathan draped the blanket over his brother and placed the cat on the bed.

"When times get tough, we must weather ourselves for future storms."

The door closed and silence engulfed the room.

It began to snow as Gregory moved to the windowsill. The wind echoed through the house as if a demon wanted in.

His breath dissipated on the cold pane. He thought he saw Christian's eyes peering from the flurries, and he wanted so badly to hear his voice. But now that his freedoms were stripped, that was no longer possible.

XX

Inquiry

Monday, January 5, 2009: 5.00 p.m.

The cold air blistered without rain. The sky was black and the day seemed nonexistent. The weather had been exceptionally bleak this year, and no one knew when the last time winter of this magnitude had occurred.

Jeanie wore her favorite red Tom Ford sweater as she sipped her coffee. She'd just gotten home from school and wondered what her parents wanted to talk about. She had been in seventh period when her father left a text asking her to come home first thing after school.

She sat on the leather blue sofa in the living room. Her mind was trapped in thoughts as Cabaret Voltaire played in the background.

Sometime later the front door opened and her father walked in. He was in chestnut-colored shoes, blue pants, and a yellow oxford. The ylang-ylang in his hair made it shine with volume.

"How was class today?" he asked as he hung the blazer in the side closet.

"Don't pretend I didn't tell you I needed to go to the library today. I don't see why we can't do this later."

"Your mother is on her way."

He poured a cup of coffee and added a few drops of local honey.

Mrs. Gerhart arrived and kissed Jeanie on the cheek.

"You look nice today."

Jeanie moved her hair over her ears and sighed.

"Mother. Your compliments come at the strangest times."

"It's either that or nothing, dear."

She ignored the question and asked, "So what's so important that we had to meet? I told Dad I have a paper due on Friday."

Mr. Gerhart moved from the kitchen and handed his wife her coffee. Her black Yves Saint Laurent blazer snugged her figure. Her red earrings matched her heels as a gold chain dangled between her satin chartreuse wrap mini-dress. Her cleavage was supple and elegantly exposed. She removed her heels and turned off the stereo.

"Let's move to the table," she said.

Jeanie felt anxious as if she'd done something wrong.

"I spoke with Myrtle this morning and she's asked for our help."

"What kind of help?"

"Now that everyone is familiar with what's happened to Gregory. She wanted to know if you and Gregory were really going to the library this evening."

"Of course we are. Why wouldn't we?"

"After you lied about Austin, and past visits to the library, she has every reason to be concerned. Mrs. Collins is disappointed that you lied to her," he said.

"He had every right to see Christian."

"Jeanie. This is serious. The Collinses aren't proud of this matter. If you were in the same boat, I would expect the same from them."

"Mom. You know damn well students sleep with professors at universities. Dad's even told me what some of the students do at Trinity."

"That's a gray area we aren't discussing right now," he said.

"Why not? If this is on the table—it's fair game."

"Relationships between students and professors are discouraged. It can distort the environment. Most times the affairs are kept silent until graduation, and sometimes they aren't. What's highly frowned upon is when students get involved with married faculty," he said.

"Jeanie. Can I ask why you're not taking this seriously?" asked her mother.

"Christian is one of the top litigators in the state. You don't get to dispute regulatory agencies with the Texas Supreme Court and the Fifth Circuit Court of Appeals if you suck."

"But that doesn't mean he's above the law."

"Please, Dad. Ivy Leaguers date high school seniors all the time. Conservative families don't think twice about that as long as both sides come from wealthy backgrounds."

Her mother looked at the father and recognized the validity of the statement. She knew double standards existed everywhere, but she knew pedigree families felt more inclined because she often dealt with them in her practice.

"All right, Jeanie. Before you roll your eyes, I agree with you. But under no circumstances can you tell Gregory what we talked about."

Jeanie felt her heart skip a beat. Their family had always been close and secrets were never kept. This was the reason she was so upset with Gregory because he knew how much that meant to them.

"Okay," replied Jeanie.

"Your father and I have talked about this even before Gregory got into trouble."

"And what's that?"

"How we would feel if you dated someone older than you. I mean, if you got involved with a highly motivated individual, we wouldn't necessarily frown on that. But that all depends."

"On what—"

"Well, if this person happened to go to Rice, or any other prestigious college. It wouldn't concern us," said her father.

"I can't believe you said that. Now I know where my snootiness comes from."

"Does that mean our daughter has no standards?" asked Mrs. Gerhart.

"Of course I do. It's just how you said it."

"Your mother and I feel the Collinses overreacted, but we have no control over their political or religious views. For whatever reason they dislike gay people—then we can't change that," he said.

"Gregory and I feel the same way. And he doesn't know how to handle that."

"That's understandable. But after reading about the firm and his credentials, they seem like a good pair. We know you two are close, but you guys have always been competitive. Gregory's ambition is noticeable just by looking at him, but that's just who he is," said her mother.

"If that's the case. Don't you think his parents would see that? His father's also a litigator. Shouldn't he see Christian as a positive influence over Gregory?"

"Honey, I think this is more political. Considering his views on homosexuality, this was the perfect opportunity to exploit that hate."

"That doesn't make sense. Didn't Josh know he was gay after the divorce?"

"Not entirely. The business climate can be uneven sometimes. Especially in the legal world. So I'm sure Christian kept that from him."

"But when you work closely with someone, don't you eventually know who they are?" asked Jeanie.

"This is where youth comes into play. That's why we tell you to be careful who you trust. Besides, Christian and Josh had their own firms, and from what Myrtle said they didn't always work with one another."

"I see."

"So that's why we don't want you telling Gregory this. Because to hear how some parents actually want their gay child to find happiness will only hurt him," said her mother.

"I can't believe I used to think his parents were decent. But now they repulse me. He and I are just glad the school year is almost over. Soon the acceptance letters will be going out and we both can be on our own."

"To a degree," said her father.

"You know what I mean."

"We have to respect the Collinses' wishes even though we don't agree with them. But from now on every time you get together, she and I will check in with one another."

"Fine. Just as long as you don't keep us from hanging out."

"I don't think that will be a problem. You can call Gregory so you guys can knock out that paper."

XXI

SILENCE

Monday, January 5, 2009: 7.00 p.m.

Silence was golden in the room of aisles that lined the fourth floor with political science. Individuals walked past their table as Gregory and Jeanie studied. They wore black cashmere sweaters with dark blue jeans. The laptop screens illuminated their faces as they concentrated.

Jeanie tossed her hair and said in a low voice, "I can't believe Mrs. Canning gave us this assignment today."

"I know. But it's not due till Friday."

"There's also a trig exam on Wednesday to worry about."

"Well, you better get a move-on because the day's almost over."

"But being with you sounded more exciting."

Gregory smiled and said, "I hear you on that one."

Jeanie removed the assignment from her folder and read it.

"Do you think everyone understands this?"

"Couldn't tell you," as Gregory opened his binder. "Mrs. Canning said her cousin in New Hampshire died from a heroin overdose last month. His family had no idea he was addicted to prescription painkillers."

"She seemed so sad when she told us."

"Since the majority of us are going to out-of-state schools, she wanted us to know what's going on out there."

"Well apparently there is an epidemic out there. Her talk today sounded urgent."

"I wasn't surprised when she said the use of nonmedical opioid painkillers costs insurance companies seventy-two billion in annual health care costs," she said.

"It's depressing to think there's this undertow swallowing people because the job market is so unstable right now."

"Do you think things will change now that Obama is in charge?"

"I don't know. There's a lot of uncertainty right now. People are under a lot of pressure, and if things don't change—they'll seek answers anywhere. Even if it's in a demagogue."

"My mother always says desperation is a form of madness when there's nothing left to lose."

"She has a point. So let's hope you and I land a solid job after college."

They drowned themselves for an hour as they sought statistics. The smell of the library was energizing in the dark hardwood furniture hall. Their hands were cold as they jotted notes on the screens.

"Over the years family doctors, osteopaths, and nurse practitioners have been pushing methadone because insurance plans like how it's cheaper than OxyContin," he said.

"How awful."

"What's worse is that people don't know how strong it is."

They continued reading as the elevators chimed from the downstairs lobby.

"Did you read how the Drug Enforcement Administration said prescriptions increased seven hundred percent from 1998 to 2006?" she said.

"Yeah. And it's only going to increase."

"Interesting. Don't you think?"

"It seems like a lot of this abuse was waiting to overflow."

"I agree, because back in 2007, Florida's Medical Commission found that out of all the deaths caused by illicit drugs combined. Prescription painkillers were always three times higher," she said.

"I think we're reading the same article."

"Why?"

"Well, it also says when Florida analyzed 168,900 autopsies. They found that cocaine, heroin, and methamphetamines were responsible for 989 deaths. While legal opioids accounted for 2,328 deaths," he said.

"What's more striking about that is rural areas are experiencing this rather than cities."

A loud sigh erupted from Jeanie as her phone vibrated.

"Hello?"

Gregory could hear her mother's voice. "What time you coming home?"—"You know the library doesn't close till ten."—"Yes he's with me."—"Come see for yourself"—"Mother, if you don't mind. I'm trying to study."—"Okay. I'm hanging up now."

She rolled her eyes and put the phone in her bag.

"Mommy troubles," said Gregory.

"She's been paranoid ever since she spoke to your mom."

"Don't remind me. They're now checking my mileage. They've gone completely crazy."

"We can talk about that later. Now where were we?"

They stared at their screen once more while voices quietly echoed through the aisles.

"To add to your comment. The National Drug Intelligence Center says high-quality heroin has hit the New York suburbs, where consumers can buy a tenth of a gram for seven dollars," she said.

"You can't get cheaper than that."

"No kidding."

"The University of Michigan also noted the spike in drug use when their national survey found 2.4 percent of high school seniors experimented with heroin in 2000—the highest figures since the mid-'70s," he said.

"Well if you think that's impressive. In 2005 the International Narcotics Control Board reported how the United States accounted for eighty-five to ninety-nine percent of the global consumption of oxycodone and hydrocodone."

"Seems like we have quite the appetite for painkillers."

"Now I see why Mrs. Canning wanted us to research this. There's a lot of tension people aren't talking about. So I guess they're searching for reprieve until something gives."

"That's no excuse to succumb to something that'll only magnify reality once the effect wears off," he said.

Gregory thought about his night at the club and realized how easy it was to lose yourself when everything around you was falling apart. He remembered when Jeanie asked how his trip went, he couldn't tell her what really happened because he didn't want to disappoint her since they had the same views on drugs.

The intercom interrupted the silence and a female voice filled the establishment.

"Attention, guests. The library will be closing in one hour. If you need assistance with library-use materials, please visit the circulation desk on the first floor."

"I think we have enough material for now. Ready for a break?" asked Jeanie.

"Yeah."

They closed their laptops and slid them into their bags.

"I saw that your dad's firm got national coverage again about another scandalous case that has everyone talking," she said.

"Anything to make them uncomfortable. I warned them not to do this. But my dad always has to be right even if cases bring bad publicity."

"It sucks that some of the kids are giving you a hard time now."

"That's only natural," he said.

"But it didn't help that Logan and Tanner told everyone at school before the news broke."

"Virginia is a nosy cunt who needs to tell her kids to mind their business."

"I bet she's proud they told everyone on the varsity basketball team. Gossip must run naturally in that family."

"Well, if it wasn't for them. I would've never found out Virginia ratted on us."

"Is your mom still talking with her?"

"Once the story broke, I overheard my parents mention that Virginia and other friends weren't calling anymore."

"When is the trial?"

"Next month."

"Have you had contact with him?"

"They canceled the Internet on my phone. I can only use it for calls—that way they can monitor it."

"Yeah. My dad said it was imperative you not use my phone because he doesn't want to be involved with collusion."

"I know you've covered for me in the past. But this time I won't ask you to draw blood for me."

Her cheeks burned bright red.

"I'm sure he's managing."

"I hope so. I could've used the payphone in the gymnasium, but since I'm the reason he's in trouble. I decided not to."

"Do you feel guilty?" she asked.

"No. Why should anyone feel that after loving someone? We're not the ones who'll have to answer to this in the end."

Her eyes gazed upon him with empathy because she didn't like seeing her beloved friend travel on dark roads.

"Sometimes we don't get answers until the end. Sounds stupid, I know, but what can you do?" she said.

"Strength is a strange asset because I've never felt more alone."

"Don't worry, Gregory. Time heals all wounds."

"I can't stop imagining how our story would've ended. He wouldn't want me brooding on that. But I can't help it."

The intercom began to speak through the silent halls.

"Attention, guests. The library will be closing in ten minutes. Please make your final selections and make your way to the circulation desk. We open at 9 a.m. tomorrow."

The sound of shuffling paper permeated the air while people moved to the elevators.

"Try not to think so much about things," she said.

"I'll try."

"At least when you get home. You'll have this paper to work on."

"I thought I would never say this, but I'm glad to hear that for a change."

A smirk grew on her face.

"I know what you mean."

They threw their bags over their shoulders and walked down the stairs.

The elevator parted and the stale air engulfed their senses. When it closed, they stared at their reflections in the brass.

XXII

Doomsday

Tuesday, February 10, 2009: 6.30 a.m.

The fog hung in the air like a veil of doom. Everything was covered in snow—making it difficult to know if I was dreaming.

But even though I stayed up staring at the ceiling all night. I wasn't tired. My anxiety was waiting for this day ever since the scandal began.

Miranda and I had been on speaking terms before the rumors spread that I was caught associating with a teenager, so she gave me the benefit of the doubt.

But once the news broke that a trial had been set, it wasn't long until an injunction came my way. I was heartbroken that she was never going to speak with me again, and that I could no longer visit or speak with Timothy until he was eighteen. I didn't blame her for this because she wasn't the only one avoiding me. I couldn't image my son wanting to speak with me after he turned eighteen, but if he did, I wouldn't push him away.

I brewed some organic Skullcap tea and moved to the stereo. I put on Winter Kills *and placed a quilt over my shoulders. I moved to the terrace and the icy air greeted me with a last hello.*

I looked down and felt the desire to throw myself forward. The idea seemed tempting because it seemed to be the only light at the end of the tunnel. I imagined it would be quick. But such a rescue didn't exist.

Life was nothing more than a test of one's physical and emotional limits. A process that makes one beg when they know the end will never rescue them. But somewhere within yourself, you rise higher and stronger than ever before.

The scars that lacerate us remind us of the uncompromising world. Hurdles that push us forward until we're left hallow.

All we can do is endure its relentless pressure in hopes of a fruitful life. So it's understandable when someone falls into the vortex of confusion— hanging on desperation for answers. But bitterness is a wasted energy.

All this does is allow people to feel torn not knowing who or what to believe. Many stand on podiums claiming the answers. But those are the very people to be weary of.

But as I stand here, I regret nothing. My conscience knows I never inflicted pain on anyone. I can look in the mirror and feel nothing but gratitude.

Gregory gave me the fuel to go through this darkness. We never became tarnished by what others thought because he was the light in this apocalyptic world.

In the end, we knew the sun would always rise and the stars would shine without us. Because in the end, everyone turns to dust.

So with that, I put my blazer on and set out
to the courthouse.

♌

Inside the courtroom, everyone sat like
mannequins. I could feel heavy eyes that
craved nothing more than to obliterate
me.

I had great respect for my defense attorney.
His black hair, pale skin, blue eyes, and black
mustache gave him depth. His demeanor was
stern, and I honored his strength for never
backing out. He saw me as human, and many
people publicly shamed him for that.

Josh's eyes flashed at me from time to time,
but I refrained from looking at him because I knew
he was trying to anger me. I wasn't surprised he
got three other attorneys onboard, but theatrics
was everything to him.

The defense had just given their closing
statements, and I hoped the jury took it to heart.
It had been a long month and I was sure everyone
was ready for this circus to end.

We were in recess waiting so the prosecution could give their closing statements.

When the chamber's door opened, the judge came in with a binder abreast his judicial robes.

The bailiff called out, "All rise for honorable Judge Whitlock."

The judge sat at the bench and replied, "You may be seated."

Everyone did so quietly.

"The prosecution will have ninety minutes to address the court."

"Your honor, the prosecution has decided for me to give the closing statement."

"Let the record reflect the prosecution agrees for Mr. Collins to solely conduct the closing argument. Is Mr. Collins ready?"

"Yes, your honor. May I please the court?"

"You may."

Josh moved to the jury box in his Oscar de la Renta suit and eagerly faced them.

"Ladies and gentlemen of the jury. I am honored to bring news that our time together has come to an end. This could not be possible without you during this difficult time. I feel your decision will satisfy the majority."

"But as you see this creature before you—this animal with desensitized morals. He seeks to corrupt the innocence that's our lasting hope for humanity. A person who spreads self-loathing so that his victims become cynical like him. How can we prosper if we let *them* do that? Stripping children of their childhood because they have a sick need to feel powerful."

"How the fumes of lust excite him—a smell only his kind feasts upon."

"As parents, we put ourselves in the line of duty to protect them from this evil. To shield them from this barbaric fiend."

"There's no telling how many other victims he perverted before he was caught. But I assure you he no longer will. Because with your help we can prevent that."

"The mere sight of him should create abhorrence. How he turned his back on freedom—thinking he's above the law because he practices it. Let us not be fooled, for the mind can play dirty tricks on those who still have doubts about him.

We must join together and banish this demon of empty conviction."

"I hold no regrets in life, but for him, he'll burn in the solitude of loneliness for the pains he's caused. Rest assured this man doesn't feel remorse for his crimes—because if he did—he would've never deviated from his duty as a citizen. Only honest men carry honesty on their shoulders. Learn from their mistakes and grow from their experiences."

"Ladies and gentleman, each of us must be weary of people who spread devastation for no reason than self-interest. If we show the world how we punish them. These cases will diminish and our time will serve as an example. I hope you will make your decision well, honest, and to the best of your ability. I have faith in you."

He turned to the judge and said, "I conclude my statement."

Josh sat down just as the room began to grow warm.

"Ladies and gentlemen of the jury, when you retire to your chambers. Please select one of your members as presiding juror. Once that's decided, please contact the bailiff."

The jury got up as the judge looked up from his eyeglasses and said, "Let the record reflect these proceedings are being held outside the presence of the jury. And all participants in the trail are present while we wait."

The bailiff later came out and handed a slip of paper to the judge.

"Let the record reflect Mrs. Joanne Smith will be presiding juror."

There was no whispering of any kind. Just the weight of anticipation as time ticked by.

When the deliberation concluded, the jury reentered the courtroom.

"Let the record reflect all parties in the trial are present and the jury is seated. Mrs. Smith, has the jury reached a verdict?"

"Yes, we have, your honor," replied the foreman. She was an older woman in a black suit with curly brown hair. Her green eyes shot fearlessly as she looked at the judge.

"You may present yourself."

"We the jury find the defendant Christian Wall guilty of sexual assault against a minor—a second degree felony charged in the indictment."

The judge handed a document to the bailiff.

"That is to be signed by Mrs. Smith."

After the signature was reviewed, the judge handed it to the clerk and looked at Mrs. Smith.

"If that is your verdict, please signify by raising your right hands."

Each juror raised their hand.

"Let the record reflect all twelve jurors have indicated *their* verdict is guilty." He looked over at both sides and said, "It is now time to set punishment in the case. Is the jury ready?"

"Yes, your honor," replied the foreman.

The courtroom waited as they left once again.

"Ladies and gentlemen. This has been a lengthy and vigorously contested trial. The jury has reached a verdict, and now they're deciding punishment. This could be an emotional time. So if there is anybody here who feels they would not be able to stand this verdict, now is the time to leave. No one will think the lesser of you for doing so. I will not permit emotional outbursts or disruptions."

Everyone chose to stay as the room swayed in silence. Thirty minutes went by before the jury resurfaced from its chamber.

"Let the record reflect all parties in the trial are present, and the jury is seated. Mrs. Smith, has the jury reached a verdict in this phase of the trial?"

"Yes, we have your honor," replied the foreman.

"Special Issue Number 1: Do you find from the evidence, beyond a reasonable doubt, that there is probability the defendant, Christian Wall, will continue to be a threat to society by committing acts of violence? In your verdict, you will answer either yes or no. What is your answer?"

"Yes."

"If that is your verdict, please signify by raising your right hands."

Each juror raised their hand.

"Let the record reflect all hands are raised."

The judge took a drink of water.

"Special Issue Number 2: Taking into consideration all the evidence, including the circumstances of the offense, the defendant's character, background, and the moral culpability of the defendant. Have all mitigating circumstances been evaluated for the defendant to receive ten years incarceration without parole? In your verdict, you will answer either yes or no. What is your answer?"

"Yes."

"If that is your verdict, please signify by raising your right hands."

Each juror raised their hand.

"Let the record reflect all hands are raised."

"Special Issue Number 3: Taking into consideration of evidence. Will the defendant register as a sex offender both in- and outside incarceration? In your verdict, you will answer either yes or no. What is your answer?"

"Yes."

"If that is your verdict, please signify by raising your right hands."

Each juror raised their hand.

"Let the record reflect all hands are raised."

"Special Issue Number 4: Will the defendant yield the maximum fine of $10,000 for the convicted offense in the indictment? In your verdict, you will answer either yes or no. What is your answer?"

"Yes."

"If that is your verdict, please signify by raising your right hands."

Each juror raised their hand.

"Let the record reflect all hands are raised."

"Mr. Wall. If you would stand, please"

I stood up and felt the weight of the world.

"Christian Wall, the jury has found you guilty of sexual assault, along with positive findings of all four Special Issues in this trial. You are hereby to remain in the sheriff's custody until transferred to state prison. You may be seated."

The sheriff handcuffed me and everything I ever worked for was gone.

"Ladies and gentlemen of the jury, I want to thank you for your jury service. You may now talk or not talk as you see fit about this case to anyone—including the media outside the courthouse. If you could please step back in the jury room. I would like to speak to you briefly before you leave. These proceedings are now concluded. Thank you."

As the courtroom emptied, Gregory shot up and shouted, "No, you bastards. You've ruined an innocent man."

The brusque and balding judge frowned and slammed the gavel while shouting, "Mr. Collins. Your son is disrupting my court. Please see that he is contained."

He flared and snapped at Myrtle to remove him. I looked at Gregory one last time as horror shot from his eyes. He snatched his coat as he told his mother to keep her comments to herself.

Josh icily glared at me. He got what he wanted. But I knew he hadn't filled the void thinking he did this on Gregory's behalf. The gap would only widen, and he knew it.

Josh's alt-right views were no longer offensive in today's world. During voir dire, the counsel made sure those views were in line with the prosecution. It wasn't surprising how these assessments not only infected the public, but also the judicial systems. We knew the judge well, but

Josh had a stronger relationship with him. It was obvious the judge sided with him.

The jury may not have known, but Josh settled large cases in the past and he always sued for damages. But this time he didn't. He was determined to obliterate my practice to prove a point since the Board of Disciplinary Appeals would now disbar me due to the conviction.

But before I moved into the corridor where I would stay until I was dispatched to hell. John had been standing by the edge of the courtroom with a hard face and a hand over his heart. It wasn't easy to guess what he was feeling, but his friendship would surely be missed.

XXIII

FAREWELL

Thursday, March 26, 2009: 12.00 p.m.

I found myself standing in front of my childhood home. The sky was blue, the grass green, and the smell of fresh paint streaked the air. It was as if I never left this beloved place.

I saw myself as a child of nine running across the lawn in a school uniform and metal lunchbox in hand. Father hollered after me, "Don't trip now."

I'd forgotten how truly alive he looked because time had a way of fading even the best memories. It was interesting how much we looked alike now that we're the same age.

A breeze caressed my hair as I moved along the white porch. The screen door opened and the same yellow furniture with hardwood floors was intact. The white sheer drapes swayed in the open windows as "Rocky Mountain High" played on the vinyl.

The smell of fresh buttered rolls filled the house. I peeked around the corner and watched as Mother sang to the tune. When she saw me, she smiled and wiped her hands over the polka dot apron.

"Come here, honey," she said with gentleness.

"What are you cooking, Mommy?"

She closed the oven and held me over the stove.

"I'm making your favorite," her eyes gazing into mine. "Do you know what that is?"

I giggled and raised my hands in the air.

"Of course, Mommy. You're making beef stew with extra carrots."

"That's right."

My feet touched the floor so Father could hug and kiss her.

"Now what do we do before dinner?" she asked.

"Finish homework and make sure Daddy washes his hands."

"Very good. Now run along and do that so you can help set the table."

I ran to my room as fast as I could, but when the door opened, I found myself inside a funeral home. The humming of an organ played as flames burned inside red jars along the wall. I watched my younger self kneeling in front of two coffins where Mother and Father lay.

They had died a week after that glorious afternoon when a gas line broke. Catching the house on fire. Father rescued me first, but when he went back to get Mother. They never came out.

I walked toward the caskets and saw how perfect, sound, and elegant the vessels looked. My kneeling self was crying even though I was happy they left together, and not alone. I kissed the metal and recalled how much I still missed them since that fateful day.

The dream ended when the iron door slammed shut.

"Wall," yelled the officer.

"Yes."

"Mail."

The guard moved along the hall as his keys rattled over his hip. He was stocky, hairy, and short. His chubby face had stubble with small, swollen eyes. There was never conversation between us. Just the passing of occasional mail through the cell's gate.

The envelope was black with no return address. I didn't recognize the handwriting, but as I stared at it my gut swarmed with butterflies.

I rested my back against the wall and waited for the guard to leave. When the door closed, the building's electrical hum stirred through the concrete. The smell of dust, stainless steel, and iron restricted my freedom, but the delivery gave me hope that the outside world hadn't forgotten me.

The letter was written on red paper:

Dear Christian,

It brings me pleasure having the opportunity to speak with you again. I bring both good and bad news, but the quicker I tell you the bad the faster I can tell you the good.

Our story received the national spotlight as people protested the verdict through social media. The scandal left my family no choice but to move to New York since it was difficult going places without people bothering us.

My father got famous through his support with social media. My mother's magazine became inundated with people wanting to work for her—as well as loads of hate mail. She ended up hiring another editor-in-chief so she could step down and run the business behind frontlines.

I declined my offers to Yale, Brown, and Princeton so I could attend the Humboldt University in Berlin. Since I already know German, it made sense to go as far away as possible. You never met my friend Jeanie, but she got into Princeton so I'm excited that she'll be able to get away as well. Our hard work paid off, but we'll see what happens from here.

Since no one in the family anticipated this, my bond at the bank listed me as the sole entity for access. Over the years, relatives made deposits so I could use it for a down payment when I was ready to start a family, but why invest in something I don't want to be a part of? So I'm going to use the money to officially separate from my parents once I start college.

The school offered solid scholarships, grants, and financial-aid packages to cover costs, so I'll have enough money to live on for five years after I get my degree in philosophy. I don't know if I'll come back to the states, but if I don't, I'll be sure to tell you.

As for Nathan, he isn't talking to my parents either, but he'll eventually come around. I don't care if I ever speak to them again because they need to remember they had a chance to salvage our family, but they chose ideology just as much as I did—and nothing can change that.

As I look back, it was a profound lesson to learn how people think. How so many lives are saturated in lies just to get their way. I feel like an old man after all this, but I'm content with that.

I feel so much gratitude for the gifts and time we shared. I'll hold them close so the grappling world can't steal them. This makes me smile because their jealousy may have separated us because they couldn't have what we had, but our spirit will live on long past this sinister ordeal.

Because of you, I'll never worry about falling through the cracks like I used to. Your perspectives gave me something precious and priceless to grow with as time moves away from us.

From the beginning I never expected anyone to understand what happened between us, but at least we found one another. They may have set an example out of you and me. But they'll never *exterminate* us because there's too many of us out there.

I feel for those who'll never grasp the concept of life because people throw it away without a care in the world.

I've experienced how adversity builds *the-self.* And I can't thank you enough for that.

I'm sorry about your sentence, but I'll wait as long as time permits. Should I fall in love with someone else, I know no hard feelings will arise from it. I will still sit, speak, and support you until you're back on your feet when you get out. But we'll discuss that at a later time.

But for whatever reason something happens to our correspondence. Never forget I hold a special place in my heart for you.

You are truly the most incredible person I've ever met.

I'll never forget you.

My dearest Love,

Gregory Collins

I smelt, kissed, and held the letter over my heart. What more could have come of this—fate had taken us to our destinations. I placed it under the mattress hoping in some way it would rescue me from reality.

I pulled the blanket over me and faced the white cinderblocks. A hypnotizing sickness drowned me as the room swelled with emotion. I no longer cared if the world took me under the surface where the light of day never reached.

ABOUT THE AUTHOR

Anthony Carinhas was born and raised in Brownsville, Texas. He lived in San Antonio for several years, but left to complete paralegal studies at the University of Texas at Austin. He resides, works, and writes in Austin.

Athymia is the fourth novel, due winter 2019.